THIS

VS

THAT

BETTER THINKING, BETTER CHOICES, BETTER LEADER

JAY WILLIAMS

"Some books are to be tasted, others to be swallowed, and some few to be chewed and digested."

—Francis Bacon

TABLE OF
Contents

DISCLAIMER / 7
OPENING / 10
STORY / 14

1
Trust / 18

2
EQ vs. IQ / 26

3
Socrates vs. Confucius / 34

4
Commitment vs. Compliance / 38

5
Agreement vs. Expectation / 42

6
Willingness vs. Ability / 48

7
Acknowledge and Question vs.
Defend and Explain / 54

8
Conversation vs. Confrontation / 60

9
What vs. Why / 66

10
Curiosity vs. Courtesy / 72

11
Leadership vs. Management / 78

12
Growth vs. Fixed / 84

13
Humble vs. Hubris / 90

14

Pivot vs. Persevere / 94

15

Brainstorming vs. Agenda / 100

16

Face it vs. Fake it / 106

17

Facts vs. Feelings / 110

18

Praise vs. Punishment / 116

19

Respond vs. React / 122

20

Reputation vs. Revenue / 126

21

Feedback vs. Criticism / 132

22

Renegotiated vs. Broken / 140
Promises

23

Values / 146

24

Beginning vs. Ending / 154

ABOUT THE AUTHOR / 157

"Common sense ain't
so common."

—Will Rogers

Common Sense. Common Practice.

We tend to rely on our common sense to help us navigate life and business. However, there is a difference between common sense = knowing, and common practice = doing. That goal of *This vs. That* is to turn common sense into common practice. What's the difference? Common practice is how results are achieved in an organization, based on the thinking, behavior, and performance of its people.

As you read these chapters you will be presented with choices. Ask yourself, "Is the choice I made here common practice for me, my team and my organization?" or simply what we think we ought to do? Common sense only has value if you turn it into common practice. So I encourage you to use the margins of these pages to jot down your ideas and calls to action for your team. Bruce Lee said it best: "Knowing is not enough, we must apply. Willing is not enough, we must do."

"Conciseness in art is essential and a refinement. The concise man makes one think; the verbose bores. Always work towards conciseness."

—Edouard Manet

Clear. Concise. Compelling.

Defining Concepts

In *This vs. That*, you'll find real theory with proven applicability in short, easy-to-digest chapters. In my experience, people use the same words but define them differently. That difference is where the gap starts in miscommunication and misunderstandings. To combat this, I've included definitions in each chapter so we'll be on the same page (excuse the pun).

About the Format

My friend Zoe is a prolific, lifelong reader and she tries to finish every book she begins. But if two books have the same number of pages, Zoe's more likely to choose the one with shorter chapters. Why? Because they're easy to start and easy to finish. And we all know there's satisfaction that comes from finishing what you start.

So with that in mind, these chapters are designed to be short. Since better leaders communicate efficiently, what we're after here is something clear, concise and compelling. When I use email I write in bullet points. The first line in your first email from me reads, "I think in bullet points," (my therapist is still working on that one). But what I'm *really* saying is, "I hope you'll respond the same way."

In a recent Microsoft article, research revealed a human being's attention span has shrunk from 12 to eight seconds—further convincing me that clear, concise, compelling communication is imperative. By the way, the same study showed a goldfish has an attention span of eight seconds.

Have you ever found yourself ...

Thinking, "Can you just get to the point?".
Saying, "Can you give me a one minute overview of your thinking?".
Emailing, "I appreciate your being thorough. What part is the most important part to you?".
Texting, "LMK, BRB, 4U, TMI".

Don't worry, a more concise communication style doesn't mean you can't also be warm, humorous or compelling.

My favorite type of work features a compelling human case, and for those who don't care about humanity (humor), a compelling business case. I don't want to live, learn or lead in a corporate world where I have to choose between humanity and business, so I won't make you do it either. Instead, I'll show you how to incorporate both.

This is a playbook for leaders. If you study it, reference it, share it and make the information common practice, it will make all the difference.

"A great many people think they are thinking when they are merely rearranging their prejudices."

—William James

A Church and a Strip Club

In the workplace, and in life, performance is driven by behavior. And behavior is driven by emotions. Emotions are driven by thinking. So if you want to improve your performance, start by changing your thinking. In psychology, this is known as the Cognitive Behavioral Theory (CBT). Seems simple, but it's not always easy to put into action.

Thinking → Emotions → Behavior → Performance

Let me give you an example by telling a little story.

There was a church that had been around for 96 years and had no neighbors to the left or to the right. One day, a for sale sign went up on the lot to the right, and the same day, a sold sign appeared.

A curious member of the church went to the township to find out who the new neighbor was. The clerk responded, "It's a strip club!"

You with me so far? We have a church next to a strip club. The church member's **thinking** was, "This is wrong." Her **emotions** were anger and resentment. Her **behavior** was to gather a group to picket and petition.

But there was another member of the church who heard about the new neighbor, and her **thinking** was, "We are here to help, not judge." Her **emotions** were goodwill and compassion. Her **behaviors** were to gather a group at midnight three times per week to make a breakfast of pork roll, pancakes and pastries for the women who worked at the strip club, to serve the unserved.

What was the difference between the picketing and the pancakes? It was **thinking**. The performance a church wants is similar to the performance an airline or any business to consumer wants—more butts in seats! So which thinking led to the desired result of getting one of those new neighbors to sit in a pew?

	Member #1	Member #2
Thinking	Here to judge.	Here to help.
Emotions	Anger, resentment.	Goodwill, benevolence.
Behaviors	Picketing, petitioning.	Pastries, pancakes.
Performance	Empty Pew.	Butts in seats.

A church next to a strip club may or may not be ideal, but what comes next (effective performance) starts with thinking. If you want to improve your performance or the performance of others, it starts with influencing their thinking.

A major flaw in many training programs is to focus on behaviors. Instead, we must start at a deeper level with better thinking to drive new emotions (feelings), which creates new behaviors (habits) that lead to new, improved and sustainable performance (results).

In each chapter, identify your new desired performance by asking: What is my current thinking and the thinking of my team? Does it need to change? How does our thinking impact our emotions around the projects we're working on and people we're working with? The answers to these questions will help evolve your thinking and optimize your performance.

It is noteworthy that many of these concepts will seem familiar and easy to grasp. But I'm not asking you to think about concepts, I'm asking you to take action and implement them regularly. That requires a consistent shift in thinking for you and for your staff as well as a shift in your common practice. Execution will not always be simple but it will be worth it.

Let's get started!

"To be trusted is a greater compliment than being loved."

—George MacDonald

CHAPTER 1

Trust

Trust = Character + Competence

Character

Intent.

Integrity.

Competence

Capabilities.

Results.

In most chapters I present you with one concept vs. another. In comparing two ideas you'll learn why better leaders choose one over the other and the thinking behind these choices. There are no alternatives to trust. You must establish trust to be a better leader, create a healthy culture and gain the loyalty of your people.

In my years of working with a variety of people in organizations big and small, I've found trust is the essential ingredient for flourishing interpersonal relationships—from families and friends to colleagues in the workplace. As a better leader, it's important for you to understand, define and establish trust with your people before you do anything else.

Trust Me, I know What I'm Doing

So the question becomes, why should your people trust you? Why should you trust your own company? We usually trust someone because we think they have our best interests at heart. We trust their **intention** (why they do something). We also trust people who do what they say they will do (**integrity**). We trust those who have knowledge and experience (**capabilities**), and those who have a proven track record (**results**).

Ernest Hemingway said, "The best way to find out if you can trust somebody is to trust them." In my experience, people extend trust in two ways:

1. It's yours to lose.
2. You have to earn it.

Life experiences generally determine how someone offers trust. It's imperative that you understand not only how others extend trust but how you extend it to others.

Who we trust and what we trust them with isn't always straightforward. It doesn't just vary from person to person. It also varies from subject to subject and task to task. You can trust your accountant for financial advice but not for legal tips. You can trust an employee to work for you but not trust them to interact with your clients. You can trust your manager to submit an important report but not trust them to solve the morale issue on the team.

Because there are several factors that go into determining who trusts who, understanding the nature of trust is easier if we break it down. In *The Speed of Trust*, Stephen Covey Jr. does it perfectly with this equation: Trust = character + competence.

To put it simply: You trust someone because of a combination of their character and competence. If they trust you it's for the same reason.

We can break it down even further like this:
- Trust = character + competence.
- Character = intent + integrity.
    Intent = why you do something.
    Integrity = doing what you say you'll do.
- Competence = capabilities + results.
    Capabilities = are you able to do it?
    Results = have you done it?

Note: We judge ourselves by our intentions while others judge us by our actions. For example, a salon owner recently updated all of his employment agreements at the same time as the COVID-19 epidemic. During this time, the government offered the Payroll Protection Plan to business owners, allowing the owner to give each of his employees $500. He positioned that money as a bonus for signing an updated employment agreement.

The owner's intent was to give each person an extra $500 to help them through tough times, but some of the employees interpreted it as taking advantage of the unprecedented COVID-19 situation to renegotiate their employment.

All the pieces that go into building trust have to be constantly considered in relation to the other pieces. Understanding this phenomenon is useful when you set out to build your trust in other people—or earn the trust of others. Rather than saying, "I trust her" or, "I don't trust her," find one aspect of the other person you trust and build on that.

It's important to understand all of the pieces that go into building trust have to be constantly considered in relation to each other. For example, a lawyer's client may trust his intent, integrity, and capabilities but still shop around for another law firm. Why? The lawyer wants to ensure a good outcome (intent) he has impeccable references (integrity) and he has a degree from the top law school in the country (capability). But he lost the trial and the client had to pay a hefty fine (results). For complete trust to exist:, intent + integrity + capabilities + results need to happen **all at the same time.**

The Trust Gap

In my discussions on trust, I'm often asked, "Is it easier to recover from a breach of trust in character, or in competence? Answer, it's always easier to recover from a breach in competence.

In 2014, the Target Corporation had a data breach that affected the credit card information of about 110 million of its customers. This breach of trust cost them hundreds of millions of dollars. When the hackers hit Target it caused their customers to mistrust Target's competence. Do you still shop at Target today? Why? Because their failing was related to competence (competence = capabilities + results). Target got bad results. But we all make mistakes, and as long as we know the other person is doing their best (intentions), we tend to give them a second chance to get better results the next time. Do you still shop at Target? Most people do because theirs was a breach of competence not character.

Now let's compare the Target incident to another kind of breach of trust that is listed as one of the top ten unethical business scandals we saw play out on the national news.

Enron was an American energy, commodities and services company in the 1990s. Before its bankruptcy in 2001, Enron employed approximately 20,000 people. It had revenues of about $111 billion and *Fortune* named Enron "America's Most Innovative Company" for six consecutive years. However, behind that supposed innovation, was a culture of accounting fraud that misled investors about Enron's financial strength. Fraud is lying. Lying is a breach of character because one intends to mislead. Enron is no longer in business—not because they weren't good at lying and cheating—they were really good at it. They lost the confidence of their customers, regulators and investors because their intentions were bad. When customers don't trust your character they leave.

A Culture of Trust

Paul Zak, author of *Trust Factor: The Science of Creating High-Performance Companies*, conducted research that found building a culture of trust makes a meaningful difference. Employees in high-trust organizations are more productive, have more energy at work, collaborate better with their colleagues , and stay with their employers longer than people working at low-trust companies. These employees experience less chronic stress and are happier with their lives, which fuels stronger performance. The 10-year study also revealed that in comparison to people at low-trust companies, people at high-trust companies report:

- 74% less stress.
- 106% more energy at work.
- 50% higher productivity.
- 13% fewer sick days.
- 76% more engagement.
- 29% more satisfaction with their lives.
- 40% less burnout.

In a 2016 global CEO survey, Price Waterhouse Coopers reported 55 percent of CEOs think a lack of trust is a threat to their organization's growth. But most have done little to increase trust, mainly because they aren't sure where to start.

After reading this chapter you know where to start. Answer these questions (use a scale of 1-10 at the end of each):

- Where is my trust with myself?
- Where is my team's trust with me?
- Where is my trust with my team?
- Where do I need more trust?

Keep in mind that trust will vary from person to person, subject to subject and from task to task. Be specific about the people, task and subjects you want to assess—don't only examine trust in an overall sense. Better leaders constantly measure and monitor trust. Better leaders know how to give it, get it and retrieve it if lost. Better leaders understand trust is the new currency.

"It is very important to understand that emotional intelligence is not the opposite of intelligence, it is not the triumph of heart over head—it is the unique intersection of both."

–David Caruso

CHAPTER 2

EQ vs. IQ

Emotional intelligence is the ability to **identify** and **understand** the emotions of yourself and others, and to **adjust** your behavior accordingly.

EQ	IQ
Is elastic and can grow.	Is inherent and unchangeable.
A great-predicator of success.	Not a predicator of success.
Improved social and people skills.	Improved problem solving and technical skills.
Ability to identify, evaluate and navigate emotions.	Ability to learn, understand and apply information.

You don't have to be in the fields of engineering, life sciences or technology to be tempted to choose IQ over EQ, technical skills over soft skills, ability over willingness, or aptitude over attitude when evaluating candidates for positions in your company. This chapter's content could be a book—in fact several books have been written on EQ including a few referenced below. *My* goal is to shift your thinking with this topic so you can make the better choice when you recruit, hire and coach.

Because I knew you would ask: According to the *Stanford-Binet Intelligence Scale Fifth Edition*, an average IQ score is any score within the range of 80-119, where scores closer to 80 are considered low average, and scores closer to 119 are considered high average. Next, the range considered superior is within 120-129, above which is the gifted range, 130-145.

Now, here's a list of some very successful people who didn't make it to the top of the IQ scale, just like me, and maybe like you and your people.

- **Abraham Lincoln:** Sixteenth president of the United States.
- **Muhammad Ali:** One of the most significant and celebrated sports figures of the 20th century.
- **Dr. James Watson:** Scientist and Nobel Prize winner.
- **Andy Warhol:** Artist, film director and producer.
- **E.O. Wilson:** Scientist and Pulitzer Prize winner.
- **Richard P. Feynman:** Physicist and Nobel Prize winner.
- **Francis Crick:** Molecular biologist and Nobel Prize winner.

IQ measures intelligence functions like problem-solving skills, pattern recognition, mathematical logic, and finding connections among verbal concepts. But what it doesn't measure is a person's general knowledge of facts and figures, like whether they know the capital of Djibouti (wait for it: Djibouti).

Your IQ is generally fixed. It's likely there will be minor fluctuations of a few points from one examination to another based on how well rested you are, whether you're distracted or not or simply by chance on the day it is measured.

There are exceptions to the rule. Recent research shows chronic financial stress can actually lower your IQ. In their book, Scarcity: *Why Having Too Little Means So Much*, behavioral economists Sendhil Mullainathan and Eldar Shafir conducted a two-part experiment. First, they asked a group of people to imagine they needed to pay $300 for a car repair. Next, they gave the participants tests to determine their IQ. The results yielded no significant difference in response to the IQ test between poor and wealthy participants.

However, when the same experiment was conducted with a $3,000 car repair, the result was quite different. The poor participants did significantly worse on the test than the wealthy participants. In fact, they scored 10 to 12 points lower. Note to self: If your people are experiencing financial stress due to the economy or personal circumstances it will affect their problem solving, creativity and productivity.

Ever since the publication of Daniel Goleman's first book on the topic in 1995, emotional intelligence has become one of the hottest buzzwords in corporate America. When the *Harvard Business Review* published an article on the topic two years ago, it attracted a higher percentage of readers than any other article published in that periodical in the last 40 years. When the CEO of Johnson & Johnson read the article, he was so impressed he sent copies to the 400 top executives in the company worldwide.

Since almost the beginning of time we've tried to measure intelligence. Early criteria hypothesized there should be a correlation between intelligence and other observable traits like reflexes, muscle grip, and head size (I'd be a genius if that were true!). But here's the flaw in the thinking around IQ: We believed and acted as if your IQ was an indicator or predictor of your success.

Here are eight facts about emotional intelligence from recent studies that dispel that thinking:

1. **High levels of EQ can ensure that you get the job more easily:** 71 percent of top managers find EQ more important for business than IQ, and 59 percent would immediately reject the candidate with high IQ, but low EQ.

2. And once you get the job, **EQ will help you to advance further:** our EQ is responsible for 58 percent of our job performance, while IQ only accounts for 4 to 25 percent of it. Additionally, more than 90 percent of high performers have above average EQ.

3. People with high EQ annually **earn $29,000 more than their colleagues** with lower EQ. On average, every point increase in emotional intelligence adds $1,300 to an annual salary.

4. Emotional intelligence is not only important for your business life: **30 to 50 percent of our total marital happiness depends on it.**

5. Emotional intelligence helps us deal with negative emotions. People who experience uncontrollable destructive emotions on a regular basis have 19 percent higher chance of heart disease and a frightening 70 percent higher chance of developing cancer.

6. Your **EQ can help you improve your public image.** A study of malpractice lawsuits showed that surgeons who spent an extra three minutes comforting and being supportive towards patients were less likely to be sued.

7. The core of emotional intelligence is understanding of one's emotions and emotional states of others. Unfortunately, **only 36 percent of people can recognize**

their emotions accurately and timely.

8. **Women and men have equal potentials for developing emotional intelligence.** No excuses, men!

To maximize your emotional intelligence, you must develop the ability to identify and understand the emotions of yourself and others, and adjust your behavior accordingly, all at the same time. If you can identify you're upset, but do not understand why, EQ is not maximized. If you can identify that you're upset and understand it's due to someone being late to a meeting, but don't adjust your tone or behavior, you're not maximizing EQ.

The full equation of emotional intelligence looks like this: You identify you're upset because someone has shown a lack of respect by being late. You start the meeting at the scheduled time to show respect to the group who was there on time. After the meeting, you connect with the person who was late to better understand what happened and what needs to happen in the future so they can be at meetings on time. You identified, understood and adjusted your behavior for the best outcome.

Here's the great news: Unlike IQ, you can learn how to be emotionally intelligent. Emotional and social skills are four times more important than IQ when considering success and prestige in professional settings. In a study of PhDs, social and emotional intelligence was significantly more important to professional success and prestige than IQ alone. We can increase our EQ level by practicing emotionally intelligent behavior until it becomes habit. **This is why I believe a leader can be made.** Where is your EQ on a scale of 1-10 (10 being best)? How can you improve your EQ? How would you rate the EQ of your people? The answers to these questions will dictate your success.

My intent is to maximize your EQ, not to minimize the importance of IQ. And when you combine your IQ and EQ, you get your XQ, a combination of IQ, EQ and personality traits. When you triangulate these three things together, you can create amazing synergy at work.

Employers are now testing for the personality traits, or "X" factor that they believe will lead to success in a particular role. It's being called "X" because no one truly knows what the traits are yet. This is part of the new era of optimized hiring. With these tests employers can identify the employees who will be happiest and most successful in the role they are hiring for and it helps with retention and productivity. A recent survey showed 35 percent of companies around the world are using a form of the personality assessment to measure XQ.

As you read this book, keep EQ in mind, and remember—the very thing that determines your success is 100 percent in your control. And as you grow and move forward, understand the need to factor in IQ, EQ and XQ as you build and develop your teams.

"I am here to help you discover what you already know."

—Leandro Sablan

CHAPTER 3

Socrates vs. Confucius

Socratic method

Socrates was an ancient Greek philosopher known for a technique in which a teacher does not give information directly, but instead asks a series of questions to spark new thinking and learning.

Confucius method

Confucius was an influential Chinese philosopher, teacher and political figure known for his popular method in which teachers instruct their students.

Socrates	Confucius
Asks.	Tells.
Teaches how to learn.	Teaches what is learned.
Student-led learning.	Instructor-led learning.
Provides questions.	Provides answers.

I worked with a group of leaders in California around how to communicate, lead and maximize the thinking of the people in their organization. I shared the following series of questions to help the leaders uncover their people's thinking when faced with resolving a particular issue:

- What was your perspective on what happened?
- What do you think your peer's perspective was?
- What do you think the client's perspective was?
- What do you think my perspective was?
- Based on what you know and shared with me, what would you stop, start or continue to do going forward?

Leandro, who oversaw training for the company, stood up and said, "Our job as leaders is to help people discover what they already know."

Leandro discovered the goal of the Socratic method. Questions allow for and create the skills needed for self-discovery, self-awareness, self-accountability and self-solving. Asking questions allows you to identify where someone is in their thought process and where he or she needs help with their thinking.

How can you determine what they know or their level of thinking if you're telling them what to do? It's your role as a leader to teach them one thing: how to learn. People learn when they gain insights from thinking about an issue, and questions drive people to think.

However, telling also has its place and there are times you will need to use a *telling* format to teach. But first, you must ask questions to determine when, what and if you need to teach. Teaching or instruction is needed when a person does not have the thinking, knowledge, resources and experience to figure things out on their own.

Asking the right questions is your role as a leader. This will vary from person to person and situation to situation. It's only through asking the right questions that you'll be able to determine when to teach. Start by asking:

- Where could you go to get that information?
- Who could you speak to who has experience in that area?
- What resources can you tap into to learn more on this topic?
- What have you always wanted to try, but haven't?

The context of this conversation is around your leadership style, not your teaching style. What studies have shown in academia is that these same principles apply.

A recent study for teachers stated: "Many will assume that teaching is more important than learning; the truth is, learning is more important because it's the end goal of teaching." Better leaders realize that better thinking drives better performance. If they want to improve their people's performance they need to start with improving their thinking. How does your approach improve how your people think? (See what I did there with the Socratic* method of asking a question?)

*Socrates was condemned to death for his Socratic method of questioning, but don't let that discourage you.

"The most influential people strive for genuine buy-in and commitment —they don't rely on compliance techniques that only secure short-term persuasion."

—Mark Goulston

CHAPTER 4

Commitment vs. Compliance

Commitment

Want to (attitude).

Dedication (to cause).

Engaged (emotionally).

Determination (when obstacles arise).

Trust (in mission/leader).

Compliance

Have to (attitude).

Separation (from cause).

Disconnected (emotionally).

Hesitation (when obstacles arise).

Doubt (in mission/leader).

Why do the people who work for you—everything from launching a strategy or running a promotion to giving constructive feedback—do what they do? Is it because they want to or because they have to? Do you know the difference? Do they know the difference? Can you feel the implication on morale? Which scenario is likely to produce better results?

If they are compliant—why? Is it because they don't understand or trust your direction but have to follow it or risk the consequences (like losing their job, preferential treatment or losing your trust)?

To survive compliance, employees separate emotionally from their work. They rationalize, "I don't like it, but I have to do it." You've probably seen or experienced this in a meeting when a directive is laid out and some brave soul questions or pushes back. You reinforce your stance and the brave soul sucks it up, crosses his arms and says, "Fine." You ask, "Are you sure?" And he responds, "I said I'm good with it." But his body language tells a different story: "I'll do it if I have to—but I don't want to."

The seeds of hesitation and doubt have been planted. You'll have your employees' mental, physical and financial commitment. They'll show up to work, do their job and collect their paycheck. But you don't have their emotional commitment.

Compliance lacks emotional commitment. So how do you make the shift away from mere compliance toward commitment?

Commitment is when your people are completing tasks and following on requests because they want to. They believe, trust and respect you. They are dedicated to the cause, and when obstacles occur they do what it takes to create solutions and accomplish the mission.

This is the discretionary performance you need and it only comes with emotional commitment. There will be times you need employees to execute ideas to improve the company as a whole even if they don't personally agree or even understand the bigger picture. That kind of performance is only possible when you have their hearts *and* minds.

Here again you can use asking vs. telling in order to gauge the level of commitment. Don't be afraid to be direct.

"Compliance or commitment—which do I have from you on this project or initiative?"

If they respond, "Compliance," ask, "What would it take to get your commitment?"

Effective leaders know the value of commitment over compliance and know how to get it. People prefer to be consulted rather than directed so effective leaders know that with collaboration comes increased commitment. What your people collaborate on is what they will buy in on.

"Merely expecting something to happen will not make it happen."

—Psychology Today

CHAPTER 5

Agreement vs. Expectation

Agreements	Expectations
Strategy.	Hope (hope is not a strategy).
Agreed-upon consequences.	No agreed-upon consequences.
Accountable.	Unaccountable.
Mutually understood.	Solo understanding.
Commitment.	No commitment.

When my younger son was 12 we had daily conversations about making his bed. As you can imagine these conversations occurred because it wasn't happening. One day, I finally said, "I thought we had an agreement in regards to making your bed."

He responded, "That was your expectation. I never agreed to that."

He has always been wise beyond his years. His response was a reflection of his wisdom—not his respect for me. This is important because when expectations are not met we often interpret it as a lack of respect from the individual, when it's actually a lack of an agreement. My son has done much to shift my thinking over the years, and that day I learned I was operating at home, work, and in life under expectations rather than agreements.

Expectations are something you want to believe should happen with no prior conversation, commitment or consequences defined and agreed to by the other party. Agreements, on the other hand, involve both parties and have predetermined and agreed to consequences both positive and negative.

The agreement with my mortgage company works like this: If I'm 30 days late, I pay a late fee. If I'm 60 days late, it will be reported to the credit bureau, which negatively impacts my credit. At six months the consequence is foreclosure, which results in the loss of my home and my credit score falls off a cliff. That's followed by higher interest rates on future purchases or denied credit. Each of these negative consequences was understood when I made the agreement.

When my mortgage company sends a late notice it warns me consequences are coming. Similarly, when you have an agreement with your people, you can remind them they are on the verge of breaking it. Your notifying them, like the mortgage company notifying customers who are late, is only a courtesy. It does not eliminate the consequences. Expectations look and feel very similar to agreements with the major exception that they rarely include consequences.

On the flip side, here are the positive consequences to paying my mortgage on time: good credit, preferred interest rates and peace of mind. Consequences can be good and bad. What is imperative is consequences are always part of an agreement.

Are you operating on expectations or agreements? Do you expect your people to:

- Be on time to meetings?
- Dress appropriately and professionally?
- Handle confrontation in a respectful way?
- Support your organization's values?
- Meet deadlines?
- Resolve conflict in an open, honest, on-time manner?
- Follow policy and procedures?
- Listen with an open mind?
- Be team players?
- Be positive?
- Do their jobs?

Agreements are a key leadership tool with built-in accountability. Being an accountable as a leader, and insisting on accountability from your team will help you achieve results. Without accountability, even the most brilliant, hard-working, well-intentioned leaders fail—they fail to meet their performance goals, and they fail to develop their teams.

How well are you doing at holding yourself and others accountable?

Here's a simple framework for gaining an agreement. If you find yourself saying, "I wish" or "I expect" those are indictors you do not have an agreement. Expecting something to happen without an agreement is the definition of hope. And hope ain't a strategy. You'll need to collaborate with the other party (employee, coworker, another department, client, leader, spouse, kids) in several basic areas:

What: the action/behavior/thinking/result that's needed

When: the date/time it needs to be completed

How: the way it will be executed

Who: the person who's needed or involved in the agreement

Consequences: what will happen when the agreement is met or not met, whether positive or negative.

Make a list of expectations you have, and transform them into agreements. You want commitment, not compliance, from your people and collaborating on solid agreements should be part of your process.

You can ask them:

When do you think we should have this completed by?

What are your thoughts about how we will implement this?

Who do we need to make this successful?

When we meet this agreement/goal, how should we celebrate?

In the event we do not meet the agreement, how should that be handled?

Once you have the what, commit to a when. Once you have the when, commit to a how, then to who, and finally clarify the consequences. Consequences for all parties (positive or negative) come about as the result of keeping or not keeping the agreement.

Recap: Agreements good. Expectations bad.

"We seldom do any-
thing to the best of our
ability. We do it to the
best of our willingness."

—Marc Chernoff

CHAPTER 6

Willingness vs. Ability

Willingness

Desire.

Choice.

Passion.

Readiness.

Determination.

Ability

Talent.

Skill.

Proficiency.

Experience.

Competence.

Years ago I had the honor of having dinner with Dr. Paul Hersey in his home. You may recognize his name from his book, *Situational Leadership*. Impressed? Don't be. I should also share I was one of 22 people there (and a "plus one" at that). At that dinner, the gift he gave me was the knowledge that two motivators define one's performance level: **willingness and ability.**

Willingness is: **will** they do it?

Ability is: **can** they do it?

This chapter is different because I'm not recommending you choose one over the other. As a better leader, you know you need to choose *both* of these attributes in the people you hire to get the results you need. My goal is to give you the thinking and skills to assess and coach individuals based on their needs.

When looking at performance, especially when agreements or expectations are not being met, the first question to ask yourself is: Is this a willingness or ability issue?

You'll have people who are able but not willing and people who are willing but not able. If a new hire comes in early and stays late, but isn't getting the job done, is that a willingness or ability conversation?

How about the manager you're consistently receiving complaints about regarding his communication style, even after you've sent him to training? Is that a willingness or ability conversation? A salesperson who isn't putting in the time or making his numbers—willingness or ability?

How about these scenarios?
• Getting reports in on a timely basis.
• Being on time to work.
• Completing projects.
• Conflict resolution.
• Dressing professionally.
• Preparation for client meetings.

A client recently asked me to mediate a conflict with a highly compensated, skilled and respected senior engineer. The engineer was well liked by clients and had a skill set few people in the industry possessed. He was also on the verge of being terminated based on his interactions with fellow employees.

I asked the VP of HR what they had done up to this point. The response: "We signed him up for harassment training."

I asked, "Do you think this is a willingness or an ability conversation?"

The VP responded, "He is smart and we have had the conversation before. He knows how to fix this. It's 100 percent a willingness issue."

I asked, "How will the online workplace harassment address his willingness?"

The VP replied, "It won't, but you will!"

The conversation I had with the engineer saved the company time, money and retained a valued employee. What he needed was a shift in thinking that increased his willingness to perform, not more information to add to the ability he already had. The answer to willingness vs. ability will determine how you proceed with coaching your people.

Have you ever communicated information to someone only to have them respond, "I know that," and your first thought is, "Then why don't you do it?"

That response is an indicator that you were coaching to ability when the coaching needed was around their willingness. Simply asking the employee, directly "Is what's not happening a willingness or an ability conversation for us?" helps the individual to self-identify where to start the coaching conversation.

As a better leader you know you need to choose both willingness and ability in your people to get the results you need. It's your job to determine which type of coaching a person needs on a case-by-case basis. In most cases there is a correlation between what people do well and their enthusiasm for the task.

When you can hone in on coaching to a person's willingness or ability on a specific task, that's where change happens, and happens faster.

"The only way to get the best of an argument is to avoid it."

—Dale Carnegie

CHAPTER 7

Acknowledge and Question vs. Defend and Explain

Acknowledge & Question

Defuses negative feelings.

Seeks understanding.

Builds connection.

Engages rational brain.

Shows empathy.

Creates conversation.

Defend & Explain

Intensifies negative emotions.

Seeks to be understood.

Builds discord.

Engages emotional brain.

Shows apathy.

Creates confrontation.

Do you find yourself drawn into conversations or arguments that seem to go nowhere? Do you feel compelled to respond to accusations you know are false? Do you feel like you have to justify your behavior or choices? Do you have more confrontations or more conversations? Are you getting stressed reading this?

This chapter will give you the thinking, skills and behaviors to achieve the resolutions that come with acknowledging and questioning.

When we defend and explain our emotional brain has usually hijacked our rational brain in an attempt to protect us. Defending and explaining is about self-preservation and is often motivated by fear, guilt or self-doubt. Regardless of why a person defends and explains, it triggers a predictable response from the other person. Human beings have a mirror neuron in their brains, so how you act will heavily influence how the person you're interacting with responds or reacts.

Studies have shown if someone is nice to you, you're more likely to be nice to them. If they smile, you smile. If they defend and explain, you defend and explain. So when an employee gives an objection or negative feedback, model the behavior you want from them. As Gandhi said, "Be the change you want to see."

Acknowledging and questioning will get results that are more favorable, forward-looking and productive. However, watch your words because there's a difference between acknowledging and validating.

Acknowledgement does not require you to agree with something. But it does show you recognize the sensitivity or urgency of the situation. If someone says, "This is so stressful," responding with, "I can see this is all-consuming for you," is acknowledgement. On the other hand, responding with, "I know this is stressful," is validation, even though you may not feel the statement is true.

But at the end of the day, we're all trying to sell something— our product, service, trust, beliefs, values, leadership, etc. We inevitably encounter objections that we feel compelled to defend and explain.

Below are examples of how you can acknowledge and question rather than defend and explain.

Leadership

Statement: I don't like your leadership style.

Acknowledgement: It sounds like something is missing for you in our interactions.

Question: What would you add, delete or change in our interactions?

Statement: I don't want to work with them.

Acknowledgement: I'm hearing you want something different in your working relationships.

Question: What's missing for you?

Statement: The client would never go for that.

Acknowledgement: We need something to gain their commitment.

Question: What would make them go for that?

Behavioral

Statement: You're late!

Acknowledgement: I understand the importance of honoring time commitments.

Question: What would you like me to do first?

Statement: I don't like your idea.

Acknowledgement: I believe it's important to have buy-in from everyone on the team.

Question: What would you need in order to commit to this idea?

Statement: You're not a team player.

Acknowledgement: Collaboration is important to me.
Question: What could I say or do that would demonstrate a team player attitude?

Sales
Objection: It's too expensive!
Acknowledgement: I understand price can play a part in your decision.
Question: When considering price, performance and people, which is most important to you?

Objection: The economy is bad.
Acknowledgement: I know it has affected everyone differently.
Question: How has it affected your business?

Objection: I've never heard of your company.
Acknowledgement: I had a lot of questions when I started working here.
Question: What's the most important question I can answer for you?

Objection: My team won't like the change
Acknowledgement: It's important to have buy-in and commitment.
Question: How have you got them to be open to change in the past?

Project Objections
Objection: This will never work.
Acknowledgement: I'm hearing uncertainty about the outcome.
Question: What do you think is needed to ensure the outcome we need?

Objection: That department is always late with their piece of the project.

Acknowledgement: Honoring time commitments is important.

Question: What do you think we can do differently to get them to work within the timeframe?

Objection: I have too much on my plate.

Acknowledgement: Sounds like you don't know how you could fit this in.

Question: What's on your plate that's important but not urgent? What could you move off your plate to someone else? Who could help you with this?

When you get an objection ask yourself, "What part of this is true?" I've found we defend and explain when there's an element of truth in the objection. We're less inclined to defend and explain objections we do not find to be true. Better leaders use this filter as information to learn and grow. If you don't know if an objection has truth to it, acknowledgement allows you to simply focus on the other person's feelings and perceptions and go from there.

Disclaimer: There are times when you will need to defend or explain (if you're arrested for embezzlement, for example). But in leadership, as in life, better leaders choose to acknowledge and question vs. defend and explain when faced with push back. In doing so, they defuse negative feelings, show empathy and build better connections with their people. It also builds a culture of trust and respect and leads to shorter, more productive and energized conversations.

"The reason why so few people are agreeable in conversation is that each is thinking more about what he intends to say than others are saying."

—Francois de La Rochefoucauld

CHAPTER 8

Conversation vs. Confrontation

Conversation

Approach: ask clarifying questions.

Priority: seek other's perspective.

Goal: to understand.

Strategy: listen (to capture the thinking and emotion underneath the words to ask better questions).

Questions: Inquisitive (start with "what" and "how").

Tone: humility.

About: doing what's right.

Confrontation

Approach: speak.

Priority: share your perspective.

Goal: to be understood.

Strategy: listen (but only to catch your breath and formulate response).

Questions: Accusatory (if any, start with "why").

Tone: arrogance.

About: being right.

Have you ever been invited—formally or informally—into a conversation that felt more like a confrontation? Like you needed boxing gloves, a referee, and rounds for a break? It was filled with assumptions, accusations and arrogance. The other person did the majority of speaking, and was hell bent on sharing their perspective and thinking, which mimicked a late-night talk show monologue.

You got a glimmer of hope when they asked a question, but realized they were only catching their breath, reloading and adding to their monologue. And upon deeper assessment of the question, you realized it was more accusatory than inquisitive. These types of questions always start with "why." "Why did you do that?" "Why were you late?" "Why did you miss your numbers?" "Why did you let that happen?"

When the person speaking to you momentarily stopped to inhale, did you respond? Did they interrupt, talk over or even ignore you? Did you find yourself getting defensive? You're in the ring, it's the late rounds and the referee is not stopping the bombardment of punches. The combination of an arrogant tone of voice, and a focus on being right, has resulted in a confrontation—not the advertised conversation.

It stressed me out to write this, and I imagine it's even more stressful to read it. I began by asking if this scenario has happened to you. Now I'm going to ask if you've ever done it to someone else? How often? Are you cringing yet?

If the answer was an unequivocal, "yes," you have either been the perpetrator or the recipient of a confrontation (an interaction that included antagonistic forces—a fight, battle or conflict). There's a better choice—conversation!

Simply put, conversation is an exchange of thoughts, ideas or emotions with the goal of understanding the other's perspective. To gain understanding and clarity, asking clarifying questions is the best approach. Your priority in the conversation is to seek the other person's perspective—you can't change or influence someone's perspective until you first understand it.

How you do this is simple: LISTEN! Listen for the thinking and emotion underneath what the other person is saying. I was in a meeting with a company that was decentralizing and transitioning to a regionalized structure. The CEO, president and five VPs were in favor. One VP was adamantly against it. He said he would lose control of the process, people and performance and then asked, "What would be my role in this restructure?" The other attendees then proceeded to defend and explain the process over and over, for eight months.

For fun, I did the math on what their meetings cost them on an hourly basis. The eight executive committee members averaged $300,000 in annual pay. That's approximately $150/hr. So a one-hour meeting with this group cost $1,200. This same meeting went on eight times before I was asked in (not counting all the sidebar meetings, water cooler conversations and happy-hour chats).

The ability to choose conversation over confrontation could have saved them a minimum of $9,600. How many of these conversations do you think this organization has had and at what cost? How many does your company have? What's the cost to you? What I was listening for, and heard from that VP, was the underlying thinking and emotion of fear. He feared losing control and his place in the organization—he could be out of a job! His significance, self worth and sense of belonging were being threatened.

I encouraged the CEO to approach his VP with an acknowledgement of the VP's fear. The CEO went back to the VP, and started by addressing the VP's thinking and emotion, and guess what? It changed the confrontation into a conversation. The CEO asked, "What control would be lost, and how would that affect you? He went on to communicate that the VP would be a key player in the restructuring of the organization. The VP was reassured he is and will be an intricate part of the success of the company. It took humility from the CEO to consider a perspective other than his own and a willingness to focus on gaining understanding and clarity by asking clarifying questions to achieve the breakthrough. Don't underestimate how a lack of humility can bury you as an effective communicator. When you listen for emotion and thinking, and your responses reflect that, it drives a conversation that is clear, concise and constructive.

"You can tell whether a man is clever by his answers. You can tell whether a man is wise by his questions."

—Naguib Mahfouz

CHAPTER 9

What vs. Why

What

Solution focused.

Takes you to the future.

Resolutions.

Inquisitive.

Potential.

Why

Problem focused.

Takes you to the past.

Explanations.

Accusatory.

Limits.

In Simon Sinek's book, *Start with Why*, he writes about the "why" behind leadership and how it serves to inspire. Like millions of others, I'm in agreement with his thinking. The "why" I'm referencing in this chapter is different. This "why" is problem-focused and usually results in a negative response.

- Why were you late?
- Why didn't you complete the task?
- Why don't you get along with your peers?
- Why didn't you make your numbers?
- Why aren't you promoting our other products and services?
- Why didn't you follow up?
- Why didn't you get more done?
- Why don't you have more clients?
- Why isn't this working?

"Why" questions take you back in time, they tend to be problem focused and feel accusatory. When I ask you why you were late yesterday your brain takes you back to yesterday's problem while simultaneously putting you on the defensive. In self-preservation mode your instinct is to defend yourself—and no matter how skilled you may be your explanations sound like excuses. "Why" questions cause us to focus on our limitations and often lead into a victim mentality.

Review the questions above. Do you see how the "why" approach to questioning creates more problems rather than leading to solutions?

What (see what I did there?) is the solution? Asking "what" questions, of course! "What" questions shift perspectives into the future. They prompt solution-based thinking. The responses are solutions not excuses. "What" hits the brain as inquisitive not accusatory.

"What" questions result in improved thinking, which leads to a growth mindset, which is what you need to solve problems and answer questions. Let's change the questions below from "why" to "what" and watch what happens.

Why	What
Why were you late?	What do you need to do to get here on time?
Why didn't you complete the task?	What do you need to do differently so these tasks are completed?
Why can't you get along with your peers?	What could you do to bridge the gap with the team?
Why didn't you make your numbers?	What do you need to do to hit your numbers in the future?
Why aren't you promoting our other products and services?	What would give you a greater comfort level in recommending all of our offerings?
Why didn't you follow up?	What are your thoughts on your follow-up procedure?
Why didn't you get more done?	What could you do differently in the future to accomplish more in the same time frame?
Why don't you have more clients?	What do you need to do to gain more clients?
Why isn't this working?	What do you need to make this work?

This choice in questioning will lead to conversations that help your people be self aware, self accountable and self solving. Try it in your next meeting or follow-up on a specific challenge you're having with an employee. Using "what" will change the tone, thinking and outcome of the conversation.

"Curiosity is one of the permanent and certain characteristics of a vigorous intellect."

—Samuel Johnson

CHAPTER 10

Curiosity vs. Courtesy

Curiosity

Includes wording that is detailed, specific and personal.

Comes across as genuine, sincere, and authentic.

Leads to a more detailed and specific response.

Replies are insightful, useful and interesting.

Requires a detailed response.

Builds trust.

Courtesy

Includes wording that is broad, generic and impersona.l

Comes across as disingenuous, insincere and inauthentic.

Leads to a one- or two-word response.

Replies are brief and meaningless.

Answered in one or two words.

Creates lack of trust.

This chapter is about the filter you use to ask questions. Do you ask out of courtesy or out of curiosity? How often have you asked or been asked generic, go-to questions? You know, the ones where "good" or "fine" apply to all responses.

Socially:
- How are things?
- How's it going?
- How are you doing?
- How's everything with you?
- How's the family?
- How was your weekend?

Professionally:
- How's the project going?
- How's everyone doing today?
- What's new?
- How did it go?
- How's it going so far?

These questions are broad and impersonal. The answers you receive will not be useful or interesting, and they won't add value to your relationships. They also fail to build connection or show you care. And quite often they're a waste of time.

If your goal is to get better at time management, eliminating the courtesy question is a great place to start. You're probably asking one of the above questions or some version of them in every interaction.

These courtesy questions also impact the trust and respect between you and the person you're speaking to, both at work and in social situations, because they can come across as disingenuous.

If you want to be sincere and authentic, let me offer two solutions.

1. If you're not truly interested in the answer? Don't ask the question. You can be genuine in your communication by

being silent.

2. Get intentional in your question asking. If you feel compelled to ask out of courtesy, tap into information you're interested in and ask about that instead.

These solutions will help you to transition from courtesy to curiosity. Curiosity is intentional. The questions are specific, and need a detailed response. Not sure if a question is courteous or curious? Here's the litmus test I developed:

Example: When I'm asked at a social gathering, "How's your job going?" I respond succinctly, "Great! Tell me how work is going for you." If they respond, "What's great about it?" or "Tell me more," I know there's a deeper level of interest. More often than not-the person simply goes on to speak about what's most important to them. Only three times in the last seven years has anyone pressed me with, "Seriously, please tell me more."

Have you ever responded to someone's courtesy question only to regret sharing because they weren't really interested? I've had that happen to me, and it stirs emotions of embarrassment, anger and resentment. My intent is not to be pessimistic. It's to be efficient and genuine in communication.

Disclaimer: If asked with the right intent and tone, some courtesy questions can become curiosity questions. If you ask a friend or colleague, "How are things going?" in a deliberate, feedback-seeking way with eye contact, that would be a curiosity question.

Life Hack: Simply replacing "how" with "tell me about" changes the way questions are perceived. These questions will encourage interesting and useful responses that will lead to more productive conversations with your people, clients, and managers.

How

is the project going?

is your day going?

Tell me about...

the project.

your day.

How	**Tell me about...**
was the commute?	your commute.
was your weekend?	your weekend.
is morale on your team?	morale on your team.
is the family?	your kids, wife and dog.
did it go?	the event.

By developing a genuine curiosity in people, and listening to their answers, you will gain information that is not only interesting but useful. Simultaneously building trust and getting a better understanding of their perspective. Before you ask your next question consider if you are being curious vs. courteous.

"You manage things, you lead people. We went overboard on management and forgot about leadership."

—Grace Hopper

CHAPTER 11

Leadership vs. Management

Leader

Focus on people.

Has commitment from people.

People first.

Leverages their EQ.

Trust comes from character.

Relies on balance of emotional and rational brain.

Believes thinking improves performance.

Empowers.

Develops leaders.

Asks so as to help with learning.

Manager

Focus on process and procedure.

Has compliance from people.

Task first.

Leverages their IQ.

Trust comes from competence.

Relies on rational brain.

Believes behavior improves performance.

Delegates.

Develops followers.

Tells in order to teach.

In my experience, companies prefer to promote people from within than hire outside the organization. Advancement, based on most organizational charts, comes in the form of a promotion and a title. Individuals become viable candidates when they "exceed expectations" on their reviews. The super-worker becomes the super-visor. The top salesperson becomes the next sales manager. The smartest engineer becomes the new department head. The head scientist is put in charge of the lab. The lawyer becomes a partner.

But there's no correlation between their current skill set and the job description for the manager position (meanwhile, what the company really wants is a leader). At best, the company loses its top worker and gains a mediocre manager or partner. At worst, they now have a problem manager who receives complaints and needs constant coaching. They lose a star sales person, engineer, chemist, etc. and still lack the leadership they need. Any of this sound familiar?

Because of this cycle, I am often asked two questions:

1. Are good leaders born or made?

2. How can I turn my managers into leaders?

Before responding, I ask:

1. How many managers do you have?

2. How many leaders do you have?

There's usually an immediate response about the number of managers, with organization charts as documentation. The question about leaders is always followed by a pause and a number that's something less than the amount of managers.

How many managers and leaders are in your organization? Keep reading to learn the differences between the two and I'll ask again at the end of the chapter.

Management focuses on process and procedure. A good manager gets the job done on time with compliance from their people. For managers, tasks are prioritized over people, which can come at the risk of their relationships. Managers rely on their IQ vs. their EQ, and trust is built primarily based on the manager's competence. Managers focus on behaviors rather than thinking to develop their people.

Leadership, on the other hand, focuses on people. Leaders get their people's emotional commitment, because with it comes discretionary performance. They add a compelling human case to their business case and people naturally follow their leadership. Trust is the leader's currency. That trust is built from a combination of character and competence, and they know that a breach in character is harder to recover from than a breach in competence.

Science and research tell us the skills associated with leaders can be taught, which is great news. No need to search for that elusive natural-born leader. You can make a leader out of one of your own people with the right coaching. But beware of narcissism. According to a Wharton Business School survey, it's often cited as the major personality hurdle standing between the desire to be a good leader and actually being one and several studies show that the trait is on the rise.

Leaders empower their people and then get out of the way. Leaders rely on their EQ rather than their IQ and look for commitment vs. compliance.

Are you a leader or a manager?
- Do I have compliance or commitment in my culture?
- Do I delegate or empower?
- Is my primary mode of communication telling or asking questions?
- In developing my staff, do I focus on understanding and improving thinking or behaviors?
- What drives my decision making? My emotional or rational brain?
- Where is my emotional intelligence on a scale of 1-10?

Where would my people say it is?

- How do I score as a manager on a scale of 1-10?
- How do I score as a leader on a scale of 1-10?
- How would my people respond to the above questions?
- What is my strength: procedure or people?
- What do I need to start, stop and continue to do as a leader?

Before taking action, identify:

- How many managers you have in your company.
- How many leaders you have in your company.
- Am I a leader, a manager or both?
- How many leaders do you need?
- What are your plans to bridge that gap?

I have experienced individuals who are a good leader and good manager. It is the exception in my experience. I have met quite a few good managers. I've met far fewer good leaders. You can be an effective leader without being a good manager. Being a good manager without being a good leader has its limits. Use the questions above as a filter to become a more effective leader, identify other leaders in your organization and find the gaps where you have management but little or no leadership. Leaders are made not born. It's your role as a leader to develop more leaders.

"We like to think of our champions and idols as superheroes who were born different from us. We don't like to think of them as relatively ordinary people who made themselves extraordinary."

—Carol Dweck

CHAPTER 12

Growth vs. Fixed

Growth

Vulnerable.

Changeable (EQ).

Works outside comfort zone.

Open to feedback.

Tries new things.

Tries harder.

Fixed

Self conscious.

Set (IQ).

Works within comfort zone.

Closed to feedback.

Stick to what he or she knows.

Gives up.

According to the *Cambridge Dictionary*, the definition of mindset is: "A person's way of thinking and their opinions." "Growth mindset," a concept coined and studied by Stanford University psychologist Carol Dweck, PhD, and popularized in her book, *Mindset: The New Psychology of Success*, refers to **a person's belief in his or her own ability to learn and develop skills, regardless of natural ability, through determination and hard work.** My exposure to her work transformed my thinking—and my intention is for it to do the same for you.

Throughout my career, I have used a model to help me understand how and where people learn and the conditions that influence how much they learn. In this model there are three zones: The Comfort Zone, The Stretch Zone and The Panic Zone. Here's how they operate:

Comfort Zone: Where fear lives, action is limited or sporadic and excitement wanes. It's where failure is most often experienced and it's the perfect residence for people with a fixed mindset.

Stretch Zone: Where excitement lives, action is taken and fear disappears. This is where success and fulfillment are experienced and a where the growth mindset resides.

Panic Zone: Where disbelief lives and fear stops all action.

As a leader, it's important to remember one person's comfort zone is another person's stretch zone and another's panic zone. The characteristics of growth and fixed mindsets will help you determine what zone your people are in as well as where you reside.

Growth Mindset

- Failure is an opportunity to grow.
- I can learn to do anything I put my mind to.
- Challenges help me grow.
- Effort and attitude determine my ability.
- Emotional intelligence and talent are ever-improving.
- Inspired by the success of others.

- Like to try new things.
- Prioritize learning over seeking approval.
- Persist in the face of setbacks.
- Gives and receives constructive criticism.

Fixed Mindset
- Failure is the limit of my abilities.
- I'm either good at it or I'm not.
- My abilities are unchanging.
- I don't like to be challenged.
- I can either do it or I can't.
- My potential is predetermined.
- When I'm frustrated I give up.
- Unable to handle criticism or feedback.
- I stick to what I know.
- Threatened by the success of others.

It's important to remember an individual can display multiple mindsets based on the task and in which zone that task falls for them. Look for these statements to better determine where an individual's mindset is (courtesy Suzie Flynn, mindset coach at screwtheninetofive.com).

Growth Statements
- I learn and grow from mistakes.
- I haven't figured it out—yet!
- I strive for progress, not perfection.
- I'm on the right track.
- I'm not afraid to ask for help when I need it.

Fixed Statements
- I've always been told that I can't...
- I already know everything I need to know.
- I can't make this any better—it is what it is.

- I always struggle with...
- There's no point in trying if I'm going to fail.

A growth mindset is a **skill**—it can be taught and learned. And like any other skill, you can improve by practicing, applying good strategies, and seeking input from others. A growth mindset is also a **belief**. A Harvard Business study summed up their findings this way: Individuals who believe their talents can be developed have a growth mindset. And finally, a growth mindset is a **choice** people make. They make the choice to try, stumble, practice and persevere regardless of the desired outcome. The goal is to expand your comfort zone by practicing skills that put you in your stretch zone. Why? Being comfortable with being uncomfortable is required for a growth mindset.

Better leaders focus on both the process and the outcome. They give feedback, praise or coaching on the effort and the result. Better leaders choose to create an environment where to fail is defined as: **F**irst **A**ttempt **I**n **L**earning.

Sometimes even I need a push out of my comfort zone and fixed mindset. When that happens, I turn to these quotes:

"Remember that failure is an event, not a person." —Zig Ziglar

"I've missed more than 9,000 shots in my career. I've lost almost 300 games. Twenty-six times I've been trusted to take the game-winning shot and missed. I've failed over and over and over again in my life. And that is why I succeed." —Michael Jordan

"Success is the ability to go from failure to failure without losing your enthusiasm." —Winston Churchill

Fear of failure is the main excuse for people staying in the fixed mindset and comfort zone. Shift that thinking by celebrating "failures."

An employee once told me about a mistake he made at his previous company. It was made with their biggest client and created a sizable negative financial impact. A few days later, the owner of the company scheduled a party to celebrate what they learned from the "failure." His actions cultivated a growth mindset and a desire to be in the stretch zone for his employees.

Studies have shown people who possess a growth mindset will rise to challenges and learn from mistakes rather than feeling distressed and defeated by them. They worry less about looking smart and put more energy into learning. As a better leader which mindset have you cultivated and rewarded in yourself and your team?

"Talent is God-Given; be humble. Fame is man-given; be thankful. Conceit is self-given; be careful."

–John Wooden

CHAPTER 13

Humble vs. Hubris

Humble

Thinks in terms of "us, we".

Takes blame.

Wants to do the right thing.

Modest.

Secure.

Team Players.

Hubris

Thinks in terms of "I, me".

Takes credit.

Needs to be right.

Arrogant.

Insecure.

Self-serving.

Who was the first person you thought of for hubris? Who did you picture for humble? What emotions do you feel toward someone who displays hubris vs. humility? What behaviors do these qualities bring out? What performance do you think these people would garnish? Which one are you? How would people describe you?

Hubris is about me, myself and I. Every conversation focuses on what I think, I did, I said, I accomplished, what people thought of me, what they said about me, what elevates my significance, self worth and sense of belonging. (Thank you, Abraham Maslow for your research on the *Hierarchy of Needs*).

The hubristic person takes credit and assigns blame. The hubristic leader takes credit for success when achievements are made. "I did a great job! I must be a great leader!" This leader will ask, "What would they do without me?"

But when failure occurs, the hubristic leader assigns blame to others, the economy, markets, another department, the client, or even the alignment of the stars. There is a strong need to be right, and hubristic leaders will draw attention to themselves through boasting, taking credit and self congratulating. In response, their people learn to grab credit when they can otherwise they never get recognition. This creates a culture where everyone looks out for him or herself—they're a group of individuals rather than team players.

The humble leader, on the other hand, is liked, respected and trusted -Yes it is possible and highly beneficial to be all three. When success is achieved, this leader speaks in "us" and "we." Credit is attributed to other team members, and the leader often redirects compliments. When results are not achieved, or there is a problem, the humble leader is quick to take accountability and examines his or her own thinking. They ask what they could do differently and admit their mistakes. **As a leader, if you won't admit your mistakes, neither will your people. Admitting mistakes models it's okay, creates open, honest, on-time communication, and builds trust**

and creativity.

In success, these leaders assign credit to their people, their clients, teamwork and collaboration. These leaders are interested in doing the right thing vs. being right. This kind of thinking allows answers, credit and thinking to come from other people in the organization. If there's any boasting, it's about their team.

In discussing this concept with leaders, I'm often asked, "If I'm giving credit to others, where will *my* acknowledgement and recognition come from?" This demands a certain level of humility, and an understanding that dishing out credit is contagious—it has a boomerang effect.

I coached basketball for 17 years while my boys were growing up. Spoiler alert: We never came in first, won a playoff game or won a championship (I said I was a coach—not a winning coach). Coaching six-year olds has its own special set of challenges—they don't run plays and they definitely aren't looking to make an assist.

I had one kid who shot every time he got the ball. Predictably, the other kids stopped passing to him because they never got to shoot. We developed a culture of individual contributors rather than team players—a bunch of kids who all were shooting but never passing.

So I established that the ball needed to be passed a minimum of five times before anyone could shoot. As a result, the kids focused on passing, knowing it would eventually be passed back to them, creating a culture of team players—not individual contributors.

It's a humble, secure leader who will pass acknowledgement and credit on to the team. And when they do, it becomes contagious as everyone begins to pass recognition on to other team members. Humility or hubris: Which do you model for your team? Which are your leaders modeling for their teams? Which does your culture reward?

"A bend in the road is not the end of the road unless you fail to make the turn."

–Helen Keller

CHAPTER 14

Pivot vs. Persevere

Pivot

Flexible.

Negotiable.

Humble.

Evolving.

Persevere

Rigid.

Non negotiable.

Confident.

Constant.

Have you ever stayed too long in a relationship that never got better? Did you keep an employee for years, even when she didn't buy into your culture, product or service? Did you stick with an incentive program even though no one reached the bonus? How about a vendor you kept in spite of their subpar performance? Have you chronically hired the wrong people based on the wrong criteria, and never changed the criteria?

Conversely, have you ever gone on a diet that didn't work at first, but helped you slowly lose weight over time? Or, gone to counseling for years before you started feeling better? Have you nurtured a struggling employee who is now your best performer? Is your once failing business now thriving because you never gave up?

Have you ever worked in a sales organization that was under performing, but only stood by hoping they would improve—without a conversation, plan or commitment? How many times have you made leadership decisions with too much hope and not enough plan? Do you ever look back and realize you were merely hoping instead of facing the brutal facts? Insight, planning, execution, making adjustments, and trying again is how we move forward. Optimism and hope are important qualities but they can never be the whole strategy.

Do you pivot away from a strategy just because your current results are poor? Or do you persevere, regardless of immediate results and feedback, because you feel it's the right path for long-term success? If your organization is larger, should you do both—pivot in one market and persevere in another? There is a fine line between pivoting and persevering and there is no absolute way to know when it's best to change the plan or hold the line. However, there is a way to clarify your thinking.

To start, let's define our terms:

- **Pivot.** Changing direction when we recognize our insight or hypothesis is no longer accurate, effective, or true.
- **Persevere.** Continuing a course of action, even in the face of difficulty, because our insight or hypothesis is still sound.

Persevering is justified if you are honest with yourself, you stay open-minded, adjust your thinking, behavior, and/or expectations according to your current reality. It isn't about soldiering on without assessing your results, examining the current environment for changes, and updating your projections for the future. Your model may not be broken; it may just be delayed by something beyond your control. As of this writing, we are experiencing the COVID-19 pandemic. This historic disruption gives us examples where some companies' models are not actually broken, just delayed. There is something beyond their control they have to adjust to, as would be the case with Apple Computer or Ford Motor Company. Persevering will serve them well if they make certain adjustments while continuing to make computers, cars, and trucks.

For other companies a real-time pivot is required. Think of your favorite restaurant. To survive they probably pivoted from indoor dining to outdoor dining and takeout. Cosmetics, as well as liquor manufacturers, have pivoted to producing hand sanitizer in order to keep their manufacturing lines running. Fortune 500 companies and public schools pivoted toward home offices and remote learning—and some of that will never return to the way it was.

Still other companies need to plan their future pivots: Can Boeing count on air travelers flying in the same numbers in the future? Are Safeway and Kroger adapting to Amazon now that it has entered the food business? How will the auto makers react to the impact Carvana is making on their dealerships? Will travelers and drivers ever trust Uber and Lyft the way they once did?

In my corporate jobs, if something didn't immediately work to expectations you changed it or you became the person they changed. The thinking was that obstacles demanded a change in personnel or direction—when what needed to change was the thinking.

In my current partnership with a third-generation entrepreneur, I advocated for a pivot if things didn't work out right away. My partner, on the other hand, was more inclined to persevere. For example, we were not making much money in the first few years of a particular venture. My thinking was that we needed to pivot early based on our subpar results. My partner's perspective was that the business wasn't costing us a lot of money and we could afford to learn, adjust, and iterate as we developed and grew. In this case, we didn't need to change direction, I needed to change my thinking. There is a benefit to being open and inclusive in decision-making. Others can offer perspectives that include different knowledge, experience and thinking.

In other situations we had to pivot. Our original plan was to partner with distributors instead of selling direct. This included an additional financial component, going against the advice of others, selling the team on the concept and taking on additional logistics. As owners, we made the decision based on what we thought was the right model but it didn't work out. Shortly, we humbled ourselves and admitted we'd made a mistake and needed to pivot. Truth be told, the realization that pivoting would be an admission of us being wrong delayed our decision. If we had examined our results without fear we would have changed direction earlier and accelerated our success.

A common perception is that acknowledging failure can lead to low morale. What damages morale is a culture where failure is not linked to risk taking and learning. My recommendation is to shift your vocabulary in an effort to shift their thinking. I encourage you to think of failures as learning opportunities. If we want people who can step outside their comfort zones we need to support them when they take risks.

Pivoting is not quitting, it is being responsive and resilient. It takes humility to acknowledge when the original plan needs to be overhauled in response to the marketplace and to start over when insights and hypotheses are false. Don't think of pivoting as losing something. Think of it as being open to new opportunities. Think about an employee you've coached, but has shown no improvement. They're still late, they don't represent your brand,

and have shown no signs of meeting your expectations. It's time to pivot and either change the person or your expectations of them.

Decisions are made with the emotional brain as well as the rational brain. You need to factor in both to make the right decision. You can make a rational decision that's missing an emotional contribution and vice versa. Think of a hospital administrator who makes a policy change from a remote office, without including the nurses' or doctors' perspectives. Or, what about an emotional decision made by a nurse or doctor without factoring in the legal or financial implications for the hospital? Both perspectives are necessary to serve everyone's best interest.

Better leaders see pivoting not as failure but as adjusting their experiment. If you are contemplating pivoting vs. persevering, I strongly encourage you to seek out additional perspective. Consider establishing pivot vs persevere team meetings on at least a quarterly basis to ensure you're looking at the entire picture from different angles. Pivoting requires flexibility and takes humility to acknowledge when the original thinking or experiment isn't yielding the desired outcome. Persevering is about patience and confidence, not arrogance, based on the facts, experience and plan.

Here are questions to ask when making the determination to pivot or persevere:

- What part is my pride playing in my decision?
- Who else could I ask for perspective? We can get stuck in our own private reality.
- How will my decision impact my people, clients, company and myself?
- Do I need to pivot/persevere on all or part of the direction?
- How long do I need to pivot or persevere?
- Are the conditions driving the decision temporary or permanent?
- Are the conditions inside or outside my control?

Understanding when to pivot or persevere is an opportunity to build the trust you need in your leadership to navigate change, growth and setbacks. The ability to effectively choose between the two drives momentum—and momentum drives business.

"If you had to identify, in one word, the reason why the human race has not achieved, and never will achieve, its full potential, that word would be 'meetings."

—Dave Barry

CHAPTER 15

Brain-storming vs. Agenda

"A" Meetings

Agreements.

Agendas.

Action.

Accountability.

"B" Meetings

Analyzing.

Brainstorming.

Conceptualizing.

Deliberating.

If you are an engineer, work with an engineer or know an engineer you know they thrive on details—process, procedure and outcome. So when I sat in a meeting with a CEO and seven of his engineers from multiple departments, I spotted the red flag right away. The CEO didn't like to waste time but he also valued collaboration, especially in meetings.

At these weekly no-agenda meetings, the CEO gathered the team to brainstorm, deliberate, and conceptualize, which are all good things. But these meetings were a missed opportunity to engage the seven engineers who came to solve problems not participate in a creative exercise. Because the purpose and outcome of the meetings were not determined and communicated ahead of time, they were perceived as ineffective and unproductive. They were ultimately demotivating and became frustrating for these key employees.

How true are these statements about your meetings?

- We never document takeaways, action items or agreements.
- The meetings are a waste of time.
- We have too many meetings.
- They have no purpose or structure.
- The moderator isn't the best person to run it.
- There are no ground rules for conduct.
- The meetings aren't relevant to everyone in attendance.
- There is no built in accountability.

My recommendation, that they implemented that day, was to have "A" agenda meetings and "B" brainstorming meetings.

"A" meetings would:
- Determine if everyone invited needs to be there.
- Start and end on time.
- Follow an agenda.
- Number-one on the agenda: written and agreed upon rules of engagement (no judging, interrupting, yelling, ignoring, etc).

- Stop 15 minutes before scheduled end time to document agreements and next steps.
- Use "hard stop" in conversation to ensure a timely ending.
- Identify a DOM (Director of Momentum) who would:
    - Keep time.
    - Help determine what topics are a separate meeting.
    - Track progress.
    - Hold group accountable to rules of engagement (which include using company values as filters for communication. E.g., respect, collaboration and honesty).

"B" meetings were to:
- Brainstorm.
- Deliberate.
- Conceive.
- Create.
- Invent.
- Analyze.

Amazon's Jeff Bezos is known for running effective meetings because he gets everyone to agree beforehand on the outcome of the meeting. Better leaders gain agreement in advance in an effort to get results. This way, outcomes are achieved and time is respected.

Are the meetings on your calendar "A" or "B" meetings? Maybe you haven't defined them yet. Before your next meeting, gain agreement on the desired outcome so everyone involved has a clear picture on preparation, participation, process and purpose.

"Making mistakes
is better than faking
perfection."

–Unknown

CHAPTER 16

Face it vs. Fake it

Face

Confront.

Genuine.

Vulnerable.

Expose.

Acknowledge lack of plan,
experience or ability.

Fake

Avoid.

Counterfeit.

Defensive.

Cover up.

Conceal lack of plan, experience
or ability.

Four years ago I was in Cleveland for a speaking engagement and found myself with a free Sunday. I wanted to do two things: Go to church and go to the Rock & Roll Hall of Fame. For the Hall of Fame, I went online and booked my ticket, my transportation and bought a t-shirt. For church, I thought, "If God wants me to go, he'll give me a sign." Cause that's how faith works—right?

Saturday night, while checking in at the front desk, I saw a sign for "The Forgiveness Church." I asked about it and the front desk person told me the church's building burned down and was being rebuilt. In the interim, they were meeting in one of the hotel's ballrooms. There was my sign!

The next morning, I went to church in the hotel ballroom. The pastor, a gentleman in a three-piece green suit with a matching tie, preached maybe the best sermon I've ever heard. He told his congregation, "I know you've all heard the saying, 'Fake it 'til you make it,' but I'm here to tell you, you've got to face it to make it." At that moment, the pastor shifted my thinking and got an amen from me.

For many organizations I've worked with, "fake it 'til you make it" is the strategy for newly promoted leaders and people taking on new roles. For those who have taken on a new role and didn't have a plan, experience or the perfect skills for a job are probably familiar with the strategy. When this happens, it's not uncommon for people to be in over their heads for a time and combine "faking it" with doing their best until they grow into their new position. If you come off as arrogant, or if you're not transparent with people, it will eliminate any margin of error you have with your team when something goes wrong. Faking it and hiding your deficiencies breaks the trust and connections you have with the rest of the team and organization.

Facing it requires the ultimate leadership quality: vulnerability. I define vulnerability as sharing openly and allowing others to see something in you that could leave a less-than-positive impression. Vulnerability is me sharing that I didn't graduate from high school or college. By admitting that, I run the risk that you may think differently about me.

Faking it was the first half of my career—I hid my secret from everyone. No one knew, but for me faking it was the equivalent of carrying an extra 100 pounds. When I finally did share my education the reaction was astounding. Rather than pulling away, people were drawn to me.

In Rick Warren's book, *A Purpose Driven Life*, he wrote: "People impress from a distance and influence from up close." How do they influence? By being vulnerable. Since revealing my education, or lack thereof, I've embraced vulnerability in my leadership style. It's my go-to connector with people. When I share my inexperience, fears and failures, my peers, team and audience draw closer to me.

A leader is someone who influences. You can lead from anywhere and you can lead without a title. If you influence other people, you're a leader. However, *better* leaders embrace vulnerability and *face* pain points, problems and predicaments with honesty and transparency because they're open to growth. They know vulnerability is a strength. Not a weakness.

"You're entitled to your own opinions, but you're not entitled to your own facts."

–Daniel Levitin

CHAPTER 17

Facts vs. Feelings

Fact	Feeling
The truth.	Your truth.
Reality.	Perception.
Certainty.	Emotions or belief.
Respond.	React.
Logic.	Instinct.

On a recent call with my team, I mentioned we would be adding an additional sales role. Jim asked, "What about Bryan for that role?" I responded, "This role requires a different skill set than Bryan's."

Bryan himself was on vacation and not on the call. Two weeks later, one of the managers called to let me know Bryan was upset. Jim told him about the new role and also let him know he was not a "good candidate." As you can imagine, Bryan felt that if we weren't satisfied with his performance he should have found out from his manager, not by a peer who heard it on a conference call.

I was FURIOUS. I felt Jim's intention was to undermine our culture and I wanted to act on my feelings right away. I was ready to fire Jim on the spot. He had violated two of my core values of communication and harmony by sharing information inappropriately.

But then I paused—I had to make a choice not follow a feeling. I emailed Jim and requested a meeting to get feedback on the call.

When we met, I asked Jim to share his thinking by conveying the discussion about the new role with Bryan. His response revealed that I made the right choice in choosing to learn the facts rather than follow my feelings.

Jim explained, "I like Bryan a lot. He's got a lot of potential and wants to grow with our company. My intention was to be his mentor and help him develop the skills and thinking needed to be a candidate for upcoming opportunities and a long-term member of our team."

My feeling: Jim was undermining our culture.

Fact: Jim was supporting and reinforcing our culture.

If I had acted on my feelings, I would have fired Jim and lost a valued member of our team. Pausing and seeking the truth (facts) vs. my truth (feelings) allowed us to retain a valuable team member, benefit the culture, company, and our customers. It also reinforced how we navigate and solve challenges by using our core values.

How many times have you created *a* truth—not *the* truth—about someone or situation based on your feelings of anger, admiration, anxiety, approval, arrogance or acceptance? Notice there were positive and negative feelings on that list.

Have you ever:
- Hired someone who couldn't hold a job because you **felt** confident it would work out this time?
- Dated someone who had a sketchy past because they made you **feel** special?
- Taken on a client who has a reputation for not paying their vendors because you had a **feeling** it would be different with your company?
- Not taken a peer's word because you **felt** they were not being authentic?
- Rushed to judgment because you **felt** like your credibility was being questioned?
- Not partnered with someone because you **felt** they had an ulterior motive?
- Withdrawn from a project or partnership because you did not **feel** valued?

Leaders acknowledge their feelings and seek to clarify, gather more data and solicit additional thinking to determine if their response is based on feelings or facts. The leader is looking to differentiate between their truth and *the* truth.

Things get complicated when emotions hijack your thinking, especially when you feel:
- Frustrated.
- Overworked.
- Taken advantage of.
- Not good enough.
- Better than the role.
- Disconnected.

- Underpaid.
- Disrespected.
- Under appreciated.

Remember: The emotional brain can hijack the rational brain by triggering fight or flight to protect us from danger. Unfortunately, the emotional brain doesn't differentiate between real versus perceived danger.

Have you ever had someone respond to you in a way that doesn't match up to the situation? Have you ever overreacted to a situation yourself? If so, you have experienced what psychologist Daniel Goleman called "amygdala hijack" in his 1995 book, *Emotional Intelligence: Why It Can Matter More Than IQ.* You can reduce the occurrence of this hijacking by increasing your emotional intelligence.

There are emotional decisions that require rational thinking, and rational decisions that require emotional consideration. For example, in addition to creating curricula, school administrators also work on budgets and timelines. But teachers are focused more specifically on the needs of their students. So when an administrator makes the decision to cut funding for a reading program or music class to ensure financial stability (rational brain), teachers who work directly with students who depend on these programs become furious (emotional brain). You can see where the administration needs to incorporate their feelings and teachers need to incorporate rational thinking in order to get a balanced perspective.

Better leadership is a combination of your emotional and rational brain. This includes differentiating between the facts and feelings and acknowledging that feelings don't always care about the facts. Both qualities are an inseparable part of human nature and we shouldn't ignore either one. The trick is to learn to observe your thinking and decision making and then put the right combination of rational and emotional processes to work solving the problem at hand. Science has shown if you understand your thinking and where it's coming from, you can shift your emotions, which shifts your behaviors, which shifts your performance and ultimately your results. Better thinking, better choices, better leader!

"You catch more flies with honey than you do with vinegar."

—Charlaine Harris

CHAPTER 18

Praise vs. Punishment

Praise

Feedback that motivates.

Leads to high self esteem.

Creates confidence.

Encourages risk taking.

Builds trust.

Punishment

Feedback that demotivates.

Leads to low self esteem.

Creates insecurity.

Discourages risk taking.

Erodes trust.

Have you ever seen a child take his first steps and then stumble and fall? Do you remember the feedback the child was given? It was probably applause and encouragement to keep trying.

Now, imagine you made a bad estimate on a project for your top client that resulted in a 30 percent budget increase and now you're at risk of losing not only the project, but also the client. Your manager says, "No worries—nobody died today. You got this! What are your thoughts on where we go from here to save this deal?"

You know the opposite response your supervisor could have had. Both are feedback. Of the two, which builds your self-esteem? Which encourages self-reflection? Which builds your confidence? Which one builds trust with your manager? Which encourages you to take risk?

Praise and punishment are strategies leaders have been using to change behavior since the beginning of time. Better leaders choose praise, which shifts thinking and emotions, leading to behaviors that will yield sustainable results. Studies have shown that punishments or negative feedback can produce undesirable effects, including:

- Little to no improvement in job performance.
- Employees withdrawing from their supervisors.
- Lethargy, anxiety, and depression.
- Rebellion.
- Lying.
- Hiding mistakes.
- Low self-esteem.
- Disrespectful behavior.
- Inconsistent performance.
- Unhappy employees.

I ended with "unhappy employees" because as we know, a happy employee is a more productive employee. Nobody is happier after a punishment. Stop using punishment as a motivator and feedback tool to get the results you desire. If your goal is to motivate your employees, praise will serve you better, longer and with greater results when giving feedback.

Note: There is such a thing as too much praise. Don't praise your team when they don't deserve it. Refrain from excessively praising them when they fail at something. You can pat them on the back and say, "Good try" when they miss the sales goal, and acknowledge the effort even though the result wasn't there, but leave it at that.

Unearned praise can also be dangerous and do more harm to an individual or work group than no praise at all. It not only prevents employees from knowing when they need to improve, but it can diminish the impact of the genuine praise that's offered at other times. It's crucial your praise or gratitude for a job well done is authentic as well as deserved.

Studies have shown when a person does not receive what they perceive as gratitude or praise they experience feelings of:
- Being taken for granted.
- Loss of motivation.
- Disconnection.
- Eroded trust.
- Lack of appreciation.
- Diminished emotional commitment.

When offering praise or gratitude, you'll have maximum impact when you:
- Acknowledge the action, behavior or thinking.
- Explain why you're grateful for the performance.
- Detail the difference it made for you.

For example, "Thank you for your flexibility and staying late the last three days to meet the last-minute request from our client. Your willingness to be flexible around this shortened timeline puts us in a position to meet our third-quarter sales goal, which puts us on track for the year. This opportunity could ensure the team's annual bonus. Without your flexibility and contribution this week, that bonus would not be a possibility."

Sincere, authentic feedback makes employees feel valued and more engaged with their work. And the more valued the employee feels, the more likely they are to help others with work-related activities.

If you're still not convinced that praise can transform your workplace, take a look at these key points:

- Managers who offer praise and recognition for a job well done are more respected and admired by their employees. *(Towers Watson researchers)*
- Employees who experience encouragement at work are also more likely to say they are motivated to work harder and willing to go out of their way to help their peers or support their organization. *(Towers Watson researchers)*
- Managers who give praise have lower turnover rates than other managers.
- Managers who give praise achieve better organizational results.

This seems like an obvious choice, so why write the chapter? Because over and over again I see "leaders" resort to punishment intentionally and unintentionally as a tool to improve thinking and performance.

Intentional and unintentional punishment can be in the form of:

- Public humiliation.
- Throwing someone under the bus.
- Ignoring them.
- Discrediting them when they are not in the room.
- Complaining about them.
- Withholding a promotion.
- Demotion.
- Suspension.

• Exclusion from a team event or project.

I do not believe punishment creates sustainable improved performance. At best you will get a temporary increase in performance only to watch it fall back again. You may get compliance but almost certainly not a commitment. If you feel driven to punish, ask yourself: What part do I own in this? Am I modeling the right behavior? Am I'm putting this person in a position to succeed? Is this person coachable? Is this a willingness or ability issue? Have I coached the right issue? The answers to these questions will either validate your thinking, or lead to a shift in your thinking that drives performance far better than punishment.

So what's the right thing to fall back on when things go awry? Agreements. Agreements have accountability and consequences built in. Consequences are the direct result of an action governed by your agreement. The goal with consequences is to create new thinking. Punishment is the infliction of some kind of pain or loss, with the goal to cause suffering. With punishment any change in behavior is based on fear. Fear leads to temporary change, whereas new thinking leads to sustainable change. Remember that when you have agreements the consequences are built in and agreed to in advance. Better leaders identify and gain agreement with consequences ahead of time. Punishment is a manager tool. Praise is a leader tool.

"It's not the situation, but whether we react negative or respond positive to the situation that is important."

–Zig Ziglar

CHAPTER 19

Respond vs. React

Respond

Suspends judgment.

Pause.

Intellectual.

Their perspective.

Control.

Asks question.

React

Instant judgment.

Fast forward.

Emotional.

Your perspective.

Powerlessness.

Makes statement.

On a recent Sunday, I got into my car after church and checked my texts. I found this message: "I'm getting worried, are you okay?" In that moment, I realized my worst fear—I had forgotten a client workshop!

This had never happened to me before. I had taken all the usual steps—a pre-meeting, pre-call, and it was on my calendar. So I immediately called the client and asked, "What would you like me to do?" I was ready for her to cancel, ask me to refund her money and tell me to drop dead. I deserved it all. She responded, "Just get here when you can."

When I arrived—an hour and a half late—three people greeted me and said simultaneously, "We were so worried, it's so not you to be late." The leader looked at me with a smile and said, "It's okay, Jay."

Throughout the day, we went through personal and company values, and shared many stories, including the leader's response to the team when she hung up with me. She told them, "Jay is on his way, and *we are* going to have a great day." Then she sent someone out for champagne to go with their orange juice while they waited.

She could have chosen to react, but instead she responded, which required her to pause, suspend judgment and seek my perspective by asking a clarifying question to gain more understanding (remember, she first asked if I was okay). Then she controlled the outcome by requesting I get there asap and sending someone for champagne. The difference in champagne and condemnation was the difference between her responding and reacting.

Reacting would have bypassed the time needed to reengage the rational brain to think through the situation. Reacting would have meant instant judgment, rather than pausing to ask a question and respond with compassion. In a moment when the emotional brain hijacked the rational brain, she could have said: "Don't bother to come today or ever again," and sent everyone home who had come in on their day off. If she had, what do you think the response for training on a Sunday would be in the future? Reacting would have created a negative experience and eliminated future opportunities for Sunday trainings. By responding, she left Sundays as a future option so she could be open for business all day Monday through Saturday.

This story had a happy ending because of an in-the-moment choice the leader made to respond vs. react. It allowed for a different (better) outcome. When these moments of conflict, confrontation or conversation arise, there's only one question to ask yourself: "Am I responding or reacting?"

Studies have shown that the answer to this question and the awareness it brings makes you 79 percent more likely to modify your behavior. **How you respond is important because adversity does not define character, it exposes it.** The team experienced what they already knew—they worked for a great leader, and how she handled this situation is how she would handle employee issues or challenges in the workplace. This leader is predictable, and predictability leads to trust. And a leader cannot survive or thrive without their people's trust.

"It takes 20 years to build a reputation, and five minutes to ruin it. If you think about that, you'll do things differently."

—Warren Buffett

CHAPTER 20

Reputation vs. Revenue

Reputation

People.

Character.

Values.

How you do it.

Revenue

Profit.

Income.

Bottom line.

What you do.

My sister, who is a psychologist, introduced me to the concept of in vivo, which is observing something in its actual state. An example of her doing in vivo work is when she meets with a couple at the same time.

When she meets with them separately, she gets a filtered perspective of the other person and their interactions. Together, she observes them interact in an unfiltered, real-life situation. I do the same with companies via conflict resolution, mediation and observing meetings to give real-time feedback about interaction and communication in an effort to create more productive and energized meetings.

Recently, I was asked to sit in on an executive committee meeting for a global engineering firm. The conversation was hijacked by the topic of an employee who represented millions of dollars in revenue for the company each year, but violated all of the company's core values on a daily basis. He was a major source of frustration for his peers, HR and the executive committee, and had been reprimanded and threatened for years. But ultimately, he was allowed to stay because of the revenue he brought to the organization.

When the CEO was directly asked if the company valued people over profit, he responded, "Absolutely!"

But the actions of the organization told another story. By keeping on a person who violates the core values of the company, and diminishes the brand and reputation, revenue is clearly valued over reputation. And the reputation at stake was with clients and employees. Both were taking a backseat to profit.

The choice between reputation and revenue is one of the most challenging for leaders and organizations. Mike Mooney, in his thought-provoking book, *Reputation Shift*, cited a *Forbes* article where Morten Albaek, former chief marketing officer at Vestas, a Danish Wind Organization said, "We serve two, and only two masters: revenue and reputation. The trick is to build your brand and build your reputation in the sweet spot between capitalism and humanism."

This sweet spot will vary from company to company. But it cannot vary from person to person within a company. Your organization must have complete clarity on the values that you and your people will use to define your sweet spot.

On September 29, 1982, three people died in the Chicago area after taking cyanide-laced Tylenol that would claim seven lives by October 1. Johnson & Johnson quickly recalled all of its products, a move that cost them millions of dollars. But the company emerged as one that put customer safety above profit—reputation over revenue. It even issued national warnings, urging the public not to take Tylenol and established a hotline for worried consumers to call. It wasn't a coin toss in the moment—Johnson & Johnson had long since made the decision to choose reputation over revenue.

The most common place I find this struggle in a company is with their top producers. Studies have shown that 89 percent of top performers do not share in the mission, vision or values of the organization, yet they are allowed to stay because of the results they produce. What they do is more important to the company than how they do it. From the beauty industry to biotech, and from life sciences to the legal field, I see top producers getting a pass on supporting company values.

If a top performer is toxic to your company's culture, the difficult choice is often the best one. Research from Northwestern's Kellogg School of Management shows that one bad apple actually does spoil the whole bunch. Toxic employees spread negativity and often have a prima donna attitude, requiring too much of your time and attention. Peers of a toxic worker are 47 percent more likely to become toxic themselves, according to Kellogg. While replacing a top performer can be a struggle, rebuilding a damaged company culture and reputation is even harder.

Find that sweet spot for you and your organization—it's your reputation at stake. Reputation is about your intent, integrity and capabilities—not just results.

"Any fool can criticize, condemn, and complain—and most fools do."

—Benjamin Franklin

CHAPTER 21

Feedback vs. Criticism

Feedback	Criticism
Feedback	**Criticism**
Observation.	Judgment.
Coaching.	Critiquing.
Solution.	Problem.
Receptive.	Defensive.
Help.	Condemnation.
Ask.	Tell.

I know I don't have to sell you on the negative connotations of the word criticism. But maybe I do need to tell you what a bad idea it is to add the word "constructive" to it.

What's wrong with "constructive" criticism? The focus still includes judgment, analysis and condemnation. It may not be the intent, but "constructive" criticism still leads to hurt feelings, resentment and defensive behavior, which creates a lack of confidence. It also negatively impacts productivity, connectivity and creativity. Was this the desired outcome of the person delivering the "constructive" criticism? How productive is the employee who was constructively criticized and feeling these emotions?

Feedback evokes the opposite feelings when the intent is to help the receiver learn and grow. Feedback helps develop self-awareness, self-accountability, self-assessment and independence. It builds confidence in the person and their thinking, which is the leader's goal.

Getting and giving feedback are equally important. Better leaders understand this and great leaders know that feedback starts with soliciting and receiving it themselves.

How often do you solicit feedback?

How well do you receive feedback?

How well would others say you receive feedback?

If you don't solicit feedback, have you ever paused to wonder why? There are four common reasons:

- Doesn't occur to us in the moment to ask for feedback.
- Afraid of what we might hear.
- Not knowing how to ask for it.
- Not knowing what to do with the feedback.

To shift your thinking from, "I *want* feedback," to "I *need* feedback," you must first understand it's a basis for self-improvement. I recently received the following feedback from a speaking engagement:

"Although I was encouraged by his ideas, I felt he was not focused on one topic and it was hard to follow him."

"Keeping in mind the current social climate, I believe he should not make any comments about sexual orientation or sexual innuendo during the sessions. Our company should set a standard with professional development that excludes this."

"Too much talking about his wife, I thought."

"Political references are probably best not made even if neutral in intent, they can make people lose focus on our business given the current climate."

The Truth/Their Truth

Did you read this and cringe as I did? My overall rating with this group was an 8 out of 10, and they wanted me back. But after reading their comments, I realized there could be two truths: my truth, which factored in my good intentions and how I perceived the workshop went and their truth, which they communicated in their feedback. Keep in mind we judge ourselves by our intentions and others judge us by our actions. This provided me with the criteria I needed to get the audience to like, respect and trust me more—it was a roadmap for me to go from an 8 to a 10. But in order to grow from the feedback, I first had to move past the urge to deny it.

Defending, justifying, and explaining are common reactions to feedback we define as negative. But if you accept the feedback as "their truth," you can incorporate it to get the desired buy-in and commitment you need to ensure your success.

At the time the comments were devastating. So I went to a favorite sushi restaurant to console myself. At the end of the meal, the fortune in my cookie read: *He who can take advice is superior to those who give it.*

Getting feedback from your coworkers, leader or spouse

requires the same thinking, "It will help me grow." Excitement and enthusiasm will follow when you've learned to accept feedback and leverage it for growth. Let me give it to you in bullet points:

Why should I get/give feedback?
- To improve performance.
- Let people know where they are compared to your standards.
- Encourage.
- Create satisfaction.
- Course correct.
- Heavily weight the outcome in your favor.

What does it require of me?
- Being open to growth.
- Listening.
- Acknowledging.
- Asking clarifying questions to better understand.
- Avoiding being defensive.
- Never defending and explaining.
- Believing that feedback is empowering.

How do I do it?
- Ask insightful questions.
- Listen.
- Acknowledge and question.
- Own your sh*t!
- Thank them.
- Follow up.

Ask Insightful Questions

Here's a recent example of why it's important to ask insightful questions.

My wife: "How do I look?"

Me: "I would wear different jeans."

Wife: "I was asking about my hair."

My wife could have asked, "How does my hair look?" I could have asked, "What specifically would you like feedback on?" There was plenty of blame to go around (although if she's reading this—it was 100 percent my fault). What assures the quality of feedback is the specificity of the question.

Broad questions
- How was the conversation for you?
- How was my performance on this project?
- What can I do better?
- How am I as a leader?

Specific questions (use a scale of 1-10 with 10 being best)
- How does my communication style work for you?
- How are my project management skills?
- Where is your comfort level in working with me on future projects?
- Where would you put my conflict-resolution skills?
- As it relates to role modeling, how well am I doing?
- How are my non-technical skills with my clients/peers?
- How well am I doing as a team player?
- How well did I answer your question?

For more details, try these questions:
- What could I do more, less or differently to support you?
- What could I do differently next time to get a better response from you?
- When would you like me to share feedback?
- What was missing for you in my response?
- What are your take-aways?
- What will you start, stop and continue doing based on what you learned?
- Where do you need me to go deeper?

In the event you get these responses like these ...

• You are a terrible leader!

• This company doesn't care about their people.

• Pay is too low.

• Benefits cost too much.

• Bosses micromanage

• HR isn't responsive enough to employee concerns.

• Managers play favorites.

• Departments are understaffed.

• The workplace is dirty and cluttered.

Simply say, "Tell me more."

Listen:

• To their emotions.

• For what they are not saying.

• Without judgment or filters.

After you acknowledge their point of view, be specific in your response and give a personal, heartfelt, thank you for the feedback. Support your words with body language, and be authentic.

Example: "Thank you for sharing this feedback with me Nicholas. Feedback helps me to be a better_____(leader, teammate, partner). I want you to always be open, honest and on time with your feedback and I promise to do the same for you. My intention was to respond in a way that makes you comfortable doing that. How did I do (smile)?".

Ask:

• How would you like me to follow up?

• When would you like me to follow up?

• When is the best time to pick up this conversation?

• How important is it to you that I follow up?

Feedback is a gift, and it's also the cheapest, most powerful, yet, most under-used leadership tool we have at our disposal.

"In the house of trust, you keep a promise, you add a single brick—break a promise and you lose a wall."

—Anonymous

CHAPTER 22

Renegotiated vs. Broken Promises

Renegotiated	Broken
Integrity (in what you say and do).	Incongruence (in what you say and do).
Trust.	Mistrust.
Respect.	Disrespect.
Belief.	Disbelief.
Competence.	Incompetence.

In the beginning of the book, we examined trust. In this chapter, we're going to look at how a broken promise damages trust. Have you ever experienced broken trust in keeping or making:

- an appointment.
- an arrangement.
- a commitment.
- an obligation.
- an agreement.
- a contract.
- a guarantee.

Ultimately, these all equate to **broken promises.** What was the last promise you made? To show your commitment, did you end it with, "I promise,"

- I'll promote you this year.
- You'll have my report by Thursday at 5pm.
- I'll never be late again.
- I won't raise my voice in a meeting again.
- I'll stop interrupting.
- You'll have the copy for the ad in your inbox today.
- I will work out three times per week.
- I'll be home for dinner.
- I won't check emails on the weekend.
- I'll turn off my phone in meetings.
- I'll make my numbers this quarter.
- I'll call you in five minutes.

How many of these promises did you keep? As a better leader, you know the answer to this question because it's something you track. In fact, you don't make promises if there's a chance you can't keep them.

For you, doing what you say you're going to do is an integral part of gaining people's trust. What you say and do must be congruent. A broken promise is no different than a lie and lying breaks the trust people have in you.

Amy Cuddy, a social psychologist at Harvard wrote in her book, *Presence*, that humans look for two things in their interactions:

- Can I trust this person?
- Can I respect this person?

We've built a case for trust. What does respect have to do with it? When you break a promise, you show disrespect. You are disrespectful to the other person's time, priorities, position, people and projects. The other person is made to feel less than.

What about promises you've made to yourself?

- I will go for an advanced degree.
- I will lose weight.
- I will be on time.
- I will be home for dinner.
- I will read a book a month.
- I will watch less TV.
- I will spend less time on social media.
- I will volunteer.
- I will listen more.
- I will be less defensive.

When you have a track record of not keeping these promises, you not only lose the trust of your people, you lose trust in yourself. In his book, *The SPEED of Trust: The One Thing that Changes Everything*, Stephen M.R. Covey said the two most important questions to answer for yourself are: "Do I trust myself?" and "Am I someone others can trust?"

If you have a history of making promises to yourself that you don't keep, you and others in your professional and personal life lose trust in you. Psychologists say this distrust in yourself leads to a lack of confidence, self worth and sense of belonging. Do you see how these things could affect your performance?

The terms of a promise have two key components: what and when. Now that we have defined and established the importance of promises, here are three questions to ask yourself prior to making one. These will heavily weight the outcome in your favor of making, or modifying, a promise you can keep:

Why am I making this promise?
- I can't say no.
- People will think less of me if I don't commit.
- I'm a people pleaser.

How realistic is it for me to keep this promise when ...
- I don't have the knowledge or experience.
- I will have to juggle other commitments.
- I don't like what is being asked of me to do.

What is at stake if I can't keep the promise?
- Losing my job.
- Losing respect and trust of the team.
- Putting the project in jeopardy.

Working through the above will help you craft promises you can keep, and prevent you from breaking a promise. A broken promise is a reflection of your character and competence—the two things that make up trust. Trust is the foundation of every relationship. A broken promise equals broken trust. Broken trust equals a broken relationship.

But what if you're going to hand that report in late? What if you're going to fall short of a commitment to reach a sales number? What if you won't be able to deliver that promotion you promised? What if you're going to be late for dinner?

What do you do if you know you're going to break a promise? Renegotiate.

The time to renegotiate is *before* the promise is broken—not after. Renegotiating such elements as the timeframe, resources, or outcome before they are due shows respect and integrity. Renegotiating terms after a promise has already been broken is seen as untrustworthy and manipulative.

Examples of renegotiating a promise:

"I won't be able to have the numbers to you by Thursday at 3pm. What's the latest I can have them to you so you can still meet your deadlines?"

"I won't be able to have all of the numbers to you by Thursday at 3pm, but I can get you a portion of the report. Which piece of it is most important to you?"

Renegotiating a promise allows you to maintain your trust, respect and integrity for yourself and the other people. Most broken promises are not intentional and yet the collateral damage of mistrust, disrespect, disbelief and incompetence is the same as if they were. Better leaders choose to make promises they can keep, and they renegotiate the ones they anticipate won't be kept. They know a broken promise equals broken trust. They know that trust is not guaranteed—it must be continually earned.

"When your values
are clear to you,
making decisions
becomes easier."

—Roy E. Disney

CHAPTER 23
Values

We started the book with a single concept—trust. And now we're finishing with another single concept—values. There is no alternative to either. Trust and values are the backbone of your company, your family, and your life.

The path to discovering your own values starts at a young age, whether you realize it or not.

When I was in eighth grade, I got up from my regular lunch table one day, and failed to notice a packet of ketchup on the cafeteria floor. With my luck, I accidentally stepped on it, popping the packet and shooting ketchup all over not one, but four of the most popular kids in school.

I wasn't exactly in the "top ten" in my middle school, so I braced myself for what was coming. There was instant silence as the four of them stood up, and at the top of their voices, humiliated me in front of everyone. They told me I was a jackass and lucky they didn't beat me senseless. They also mentioned I had better show up with enough money to replace their stuff if the ketchup didn't come out by the next day. Honestly, I did appreciate the option to buy my way out of an ass whooping, but any dreams I had to become one of the cool kids instantly evaporated.

Fortunately, the lunch bell rang and everyone went to class. I walked alone, taking the least-traveled route in hopes of disappearing. But the long way made me late, and when I arrived to English class it was already packed. I prepared for my "walk of shame," but to my surprise, nothing was said. It was as if the Ketchup Incident never happened.

Two days later, I learned that Marian Barnes (the most popular girl in school) told my entire English class not to say a word about what happened in the lunchroom. In that moment I realized I valued loyalty. Her loyalty to me was unexpected and unearned, but she offered it unconditionally, which gave me self worth and made me feel safe.

To this day I am fiercely loyal to my friends and family (sometimes to a fault) and only surround myself with people who are fiercely loyal to me. Marian gave me an important gift. She not only offered me her loyalty, she helped me recognize and name it as one of my values—and I've felt connected to her ever since.

At other times in life, people have done the opposite. Instead of giving me their loyalty they've withheld it. I've experienced the lack of loyalty in my work life, home life, and in my community. I've quit a job, ended a friendship, and left a charitable cause because of it. When you step on one of my values I disconnect mentally, physically and emotionally.

Interestingly enough, Marian doesn't remember that day. Not because it wasn't important but because loyalty is also one of her values. It's how she lives her life and one of the filters she uses to make decisions. That day she made the decision to defend me swiftly and instinctively. That's how values work.

Values define what is good and worthwhile for you. They reveal how you make decisions and how you actually live your life. You can have many values, but it's important to discover your *core values* in order to understand yourself and how you interact with others.

Core values are those you would **fight for, quit a job over, or leave a friendship to protect.** When you can identify, define and communicate to your family, friends and employees what your core values are, they gain an immediate understanding of you, and possibly a connection. Your values are your relationship with the world.

Not sure what your values are? Let's find out! Below is a list of 50 values (note: there are thousands of values, so if you don't see one that's important to you, please add it). Read through them and check the 10 that are most important to you.

1. Achievement.
2. Affection.
3. Ambition.
4. Art/Artistry.
5. Balance.

6. Caring.

7. Collaboration.

8. Commitment.

9. Communication.

10. Community.

11. Competence.

12. Continuous learning.

13. Cooperation.

14. Creativity.

15. Efficiency.

16. Excellence.

17. Fairness.

18. Family.

19. Financial security.

20. Forgiveness.

21. Friendship.

22. Generosity.

23. Growth.

24. Harmony.

25. Health.

26. Helpfulness.

27. Honesty.

28. Humility.

29. Humor/fun.

30. Independence.

31. Integrity.

32. Loyalty.

33. Making a difference.

34. Order.

35. Passion.

36. Patience.

37. Perseverance.

38. Personal growth.

39. Power.

40. Recognition.

41. Reliability.

42. Respect.

43. Responsibility.

44. Risk taking.

45. Spirituality.

46. Success.

47. Teaching.

48. Transparency.

49. Trust.

50. Wisdom.

Once you've identified your 10 core values, narrow it down to five. Be thoughtful about your choices (choose the ones that define you, not the ones you aspire to)—these will be the five you can remember and recite anytime someone asks. Don't worry, the values that don't make the top five are still your values, it's just that these five rank higher.

Finally, choose the *three* values that are nonnegotiable for you as a person and how you live your life, run your business and interact with your family and friends. **These are your core values.** Education is one of my values. Loyalty is one of my core values. I have not and would not end a relationship over a lack of education; however, I have ended a relationship over a lack of loyalty. Take time with these three values. Define them, list their benefits, think about how you use them in your daily life. Think about how you feel when they are being supported, the times you feel significant and that you belong. Also consider how you feel when they are being violated (you'll know because it feels like sandpaper to your soul).

Values-Based Leadership

When it comes to the workplace, I do not believe companies have values. Leaders and people have values, and bring those values to the company. The leader's job is to turn the company's values into a compelling cause for others to follow.

While I believe in a singular set of values to guide you through both your home and work life, some leaders prefer to have a separate set of work values to lead with. Do you wonder how this can work when your values are different than the organization's, my leader's or your people's? If we dig a little deeper we find that it's not the values that are most important, but what they give you. When you reduce values to their essence, no matter what they are, they all give us the same thing: significance, self worth, and a sense of belonging. When our values are met, regardless of the name we put on them, they make us feel safe.

Workplace values are the **guiding principles** that are most important to you about **the way you work.** You use these deeply held principles to **choose between right and wrong,** ways of working and they help you make important decisions and career choices quickly, predictably and consistently.

When the behaviors of employees are based on the stated values of the company, you have values-based leadership. This style of leading defines the company's relationship with its customers, its workforce, with society and the planet. An organization's values are the bedrock of why the company exists, how it makes decisions and indicates its true purpose. Leaders lean on the values of the organization to drive performance, especially during times of change. These values must be authentic and relatively specific so they resonate with the team. Think of businesses like Disney, Apple, Amazon and McDonalds— I'll bet you can infer their companies' values.

Before you begin defining work values: You've probably talked to many business owners and leaders who've brought their teams together to identify their company's core values. This is a common mistake I don't want you to make. **Defining your company's core values is not a group exercise.** Remember— people come and go in the workplace. The order or priority of values can change, the people can change but values stay the same.

Examples of Workplace Values
- Accountability.
- Altruism.
- Detail-oriented.
- Delivering quality.
- Honesty.
- Trust-worthy.
- Reliable.
- Positive attitude.
- Deadline-oriented.
- Charitable.
- Respect.
- Tolerance.

When and How Often Should Values Be Communicated?

Values-based leadership requires the need for constant communication of values at every opportunity. It starts in the interview process, and continues in every company meeting and celebration, in every coaching moment, when mistakes are made and every time a person is publicly recognized. Your employees don't need to share your core values but they do need to support them.

Better leaders identify, defend and protect their core values, communicate them clearly and are congruent in what they say and do. And when your team knows your company core values, you'll create a culture everyone supports, defends and honors.

"Diagnosis is not the end, but the beginning of practice."

—Martin H. Fischer

CHAPTER 24

Beginning vs. Ending

Beginning	Ending
Start.	Finish.
Initiation.	Conclusion.
Creation.	Completion.
Open.	Close.

Where are you in your development as a better leader—ending or beginning? Yes, this is the *end* of the book. But it's also the *beginning* of something else—practice.

Anton Chekhov said, "Knowledge is of no value unless you put it into practice." Your people need you to put what you've learned from *This vs. That* into practice. We started with differentiating between common sense and common practice. Now that you have a framework for common sense let's make it common practice.

But first, does practice really make perfect? A new study from Rice University, Princeton University and Michigan State University set out to answer this age-old question, and found that while practice won't necessarily make **perfect,** it will usually make almost everyone **better** at what they're practicing.

And life's not about perfection, it's about progress. It's about starting in one place and winding up some place better. So here's your practice: Review each chapter and determine who and when you will practice your new thinking.

Will it be with a,
- Direct report?
- Team member?
- Manager?
- Yourself?

Will it be,
- In a company-wide meeting?
- During a one-on-one review?
- When you're interviewing candidates?
- Every morning before you go to the office?

Begin by choosing the chapter that resonated most with you and by putting its principles in practice with the right people in the right setting. Keep practicing this and before you know it common sense will become common practice.

When the leader gets better the people get better.

"My gift will not be knowledge. You can Google anything I say. My gift will be new thinking, different thinking and deeper thinking."

–Jay Williams

ABOUT THE AUTHOR

 Jay Williams has more than 25 years of experience across a wide variety of disciplines. He has held numerous roles including: general manager, vice president, divisional manager, regional manager, facilitator, keynote speaker, principal, senior manager, and executive communications and dialogue coach.

With a focus on delivering exceptional client satisfaction, Jay has helped numerous clients, from small businesses to Fortune 500 companies, achieve desired outcomes through his leadership and contributions in sales, client services and executive coaching. He has significant experience in sales process transformation, managing and driving change and designing and tracking to customer needs.

Jay also has proven expertise in creating alignment among executives and leaders to ensure clarity and focus on strategic priorities, process analysis, and values—ultimately improving profitability. Examining the role of the leader is Jay's specialty and his engagements, consulting and writing reveal a lifetime of insight.

Jay is also the author of the book *Leave Your Mark: The Thinking, Skills and Behaviors of Influencers.* A frequent speaker at industry events, his warm, humorous—and sometimes irreverent—style engages audiences, gives them confidence, and shifts their thinking. He understands challenges and opportunities from their point of view and draws on his rich experience to help them unlock their potential and fuel their passion.

Made in the USA
Monee, IL
12 May 2021

68446705R10089